LEADING AN ORGANIZATION

─── TRAINING GUIDE ───

Developing the Character and Competency to
Lead a Church, Nonprofit, or Business

Mac Lake & Rick Duncan

100
MOVEMENTS
PUBLISHING

First published in 2023 by 100 Movements Publishing

Copyright © 2023 by Mac Lake and Rick Duncan

All rights reserved. No portion of this book may be reproduced or transmitted in any form or by any means, electronic or mechanical, including photocopying, recording, or by any information storage and retrieval system, without permission in writing from the authors. The only exception is brief quotations in printed reviews.

The authors have no responsibility for the persistence or accuracy of URLs for external or third-party internet websites referred to in this book, and do not guarantee that any content on such websites is, or will remain, accurate or appropriate.

Some names have been changed to protect the privacy of individuals and organizations.

All Scripture quotations, unless otherwise indicated, are taken from the Holy Bible, New International Version®, NIV®. Copyright ©1973, 1978, 1984, 2011 by Biblica, Inc.™ Used by permission of Zondervan. All rights reserved worldwide. www.zondervan.com. The "NIV" and "New International Version" are trademarks registered in the United States Patent and Trademark Office by Biblica, Inc.™

Scripture quotations marked ESV are from the ESV Bible (The Holy Bible, English Standard Version), 2001 by Crossway, a publishing ministry of Good News Publishers. Used by permission. All rights reserved. The ESV text may not be quoted in any publication made available to the public by a Creative Commons license. The ESV may not be translated in whole or in part into any other language.

ISBN 978-1-955142-47-2 (print)
ISBN 978-1-955142-48-9 (ebook)

100 Movements Publishing
An imprint of Movement Leaders Collective
Richmond, Virginia

www.100Mpublishing.com
www.movementleaderscollective.com

Howard

Contents

Preface	*vii*
Before You Begin	*xi*
Overview of Modules	*xvii*
Module 1: Perseverance	1
Module 2: Shaping Culture	35
Module 3: Casting Vision	65
Module 4: Teaching	109
Module 5: Financial Stewardship	143
Module 6: Leading Change	183
Module 7: Review Your Progress	215
For the Trainer	*241*
About the Authors	*275*

Preface

Welcome to *Leading an Organization: Developing the Character and Competency to Lead a Church, Nonprofit, or Business*. This is your opportunity to advance in your development so that you learn both the character and the competency necessary to lead an organization effectively.

I've dreamed of writing this type of training book for years because so much training material either focuses solely on leadership competencies *or* on the character of the leader. Over the years, I've watched leaders grow in their leadership but then be "taken out" because of a flaw in their character. Conversely, I've seen leaders who are godly men or women but are unable to mobilize people because of a lack of leadership competency.

As we develop leaders, then, we must help them grow in both character and competency. One of my favorite Bible verses is Psalm 78:72: "David shepherded them with integrity of heart; with skillful hands he led them." David was a great leader because he had both leadership skills and leadership spirit. When a leader has both, he or she is able to unite people and mobilize them to make a kingdom impact. So I wanted to provide something that helps leaders grow in both character and competency.

The Discipling Leaders Series is a training resource for churches and organizations that are building a pipeline to draw new leaders from within and develop them along an intentional pathway of personal and professional growth. Each level of the leadership pipeline corresponds to a broader scope of responsibility and greater spiritual maturity.

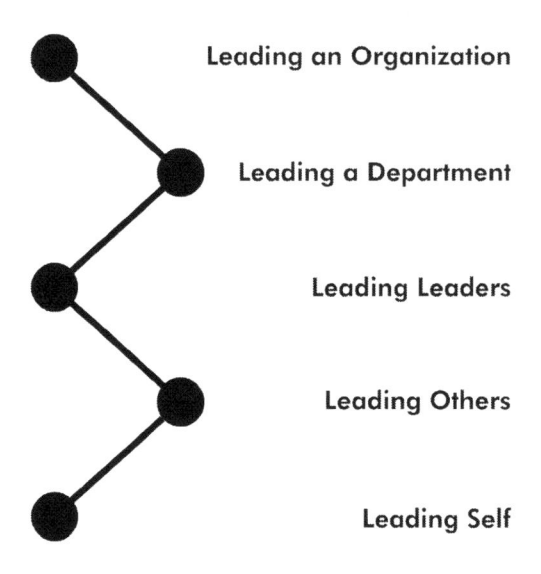

Leading an Organization

Leading a Department

Leading Leaders

Leading Others

Leading Self

The leadership pipeline in a church begins with leading self. This is where the majority of people will be in the average congregation. Most churches utilize small groups, Sunday School, or one-on-one mentoring to disciple those who are learning to lead themselves. While this is a critical step in every believer's journey, the scope of this series is not to cover the aspect of leading self. In my experience, many churches struggle with the discipleship of leaders. Therefore this series will focus on the discipleship of leaders at the various levels of the pipeline in the church.

Leading an Organization is the final book in the Discipling Leaders Series. Each level has specific skill sets and character traits that must be mastered in order to have a full range of expertise before moving to another leadership level:

Leading Self
Leading Others
Leading Leaders
Leading a Department
Leading an Organization

I've discovered that most organizations structure for function, but they never think about structuring for development. The leadership pipeline framework gives a strategy for developing leaders from within your church rather than having to hire externally. We have often defaulted to the easy route of "buying" leaders from the outside rather than building leaders from within. The Discipling Leaders Series helps equip those who have the call, the character, and the competencies to move to new levels of leadership in your church. (You can learn more about building a leadership pipeline for your church or organization in one of my previous books, *The Multiplication Effect*, or by contacting me at multiplygroup.org.)

In this final book of the Discipling Leader series, I am thrilled to introduce a special coauthor who has brought immense value to this project. As we reach the culmination of this series, it has been a rewarding journey to witness how these books have been embraced by churches, nonprofits, and businesses, assisting them in developing leaders across different levels of their leadership pipeline.

When I contemplated collaborating on this final installment, I knew that it had to be someone extraordinary—someone with a wealth of experience, unwavering character, and a profound dedication to their faith. That's why I approached my dear friend Rick Duncan, founding pastor of Cuyahoga Valley Church (CVC), where he has served for over thirty-five years. Rick also has the heart of a coach and has been a mentor to countless young leaders, equipping them to establish new churches all across the US.

Rick's pastoral spirit, deep-rooted character, and sincere devotion to Jesus make him the ideal coauthor for this book. I am honored to have him by my side as we delve into the competencies and profound responsibilities of leading an organization.

As we embarked on this writing journey, Rick and I were acutely aware of the vast scope of leading an organization and the challenges it entails. While it's impossible to cover every aspect in this book, we intend to provide you with essential competencies that will enable you to identify potential leaders and prepare them for the privilege of leading an organization.

Our sincere hope is that the content within these pages will serve you well, whether you are raising up future senior or executive pastors, nurturing visionary minds to establish impactful businesses or nonprofits that contribute to the kingdom, or fostering the growth of new church leaders within your congregation.

May this final book in the Discipling Leaders Series be a guiding light on your leadership journey, and may the wisdom and insights shared here inspire you to lead with integrity, compassion, and a steadfast commitment to God's purposes.

Thank you for joining us on this expedition of growth and leadership development. Together, let us strive to create a lasting and positive impact in the lives of those we serve and the organizations we lead.

Mac Lake

Before You Begin

What Makes This Training Guide Unique?

1. An Apprenticeship Approach

This training requires the assistance and accountability of a trainer, normally someone your church leadership designates. Although you will work through the content of each module on your own, you will discuss your responses and reflections with a trainer. The trainer functions as both a mentor and a model of the core character traits and competencies needed to develop the next level of leadership. You will learn and grow under their leadership as they observe your strengths and speak into your specific growth areas. In each module you will be required to put into practice the principles you're learning. The trainer will give you opportunities to practice in the context of their leadership role by sharing some responsibilities and leadership tasks with you—it is intended to be an apprenticeship approach to your development. This guide can be worked through with up to two others meeting with you and your trainer as a small learning cohort. Having other learners beside you in the process will significantly increase your learning as together you discuss your insights and discoveries along the way. This team approach is a return to the ancient form of mentoring that Jesus used with his disciples.

TRAINER: Please see **For the Trainer** on page 241.

2. A Focus on Character and Competency

In each module, the focus is on two elements of leadership: deepening your *character* and developing your *competency*. The principle behind this structure is to develop the skills of a leader in sync with the soul of a true leader. When you operate both in tandem, your character can accommodate the acquisition of skills and can execute them in a godly manner that honors the principles taught in God's Word.

What Is the Philosophy of This Training?

This training is designed to produce transformation in your skills, not just help you absorb information. Lots of time and thought went into the structure of this material. I believe transformation happens in a triad of development with three overlapping factors.

1. Knowledge

In order to develop specific competencies, you need to learn key information about how to actually do the associated skills.

For example, if I wanted to improve my golf swing, I could buy a golf magazine featuring an article on the five steps to the perfect swing. After reading and digesting the information, does it improve my swing? Not really. It does, however, give me some good information on the skills of a good swing.

2. Experience

If you want to experience transformation in your leadership character or competencies, you must put that competency into practice. That's where learning really begins to accelerate. It's the experience that allows you to see where you're strong and where you need to grow. It's practice that produces failure and frustration, and that's a good thing because it raises questions, which then leads to greater learning.

Practice can also lead to success, which produces greater levels of learning and confidence in that particular leadership skill.

Let's go back to my golf example. I'm trying to improve my golf swing. I read the article on the five steps to the perfect golf swing. That gives me the knowledge. But then I need experience. So I grab a nine iron, go to my backyard, and swing a thousand times. Now, does that improve my swing? Not necessarily. If I'm doing things the right way, I may improve. But it may make things worse if I'm swinging incorrectly. When I make the same mistake repeatedly, I am reinforcing a bad habit.

3. Coaching

In order to develop your leadership competencies, you also need someone to observe you in action, give you feedback, and discuss what you are learning in the process. The coaching portion is where learning is solidified. The trainer/coach can give further assignments, which can lead to further practice, which will lead to further growth. Once again, let's go back to improving my golf swing. So far I have read the article and practiced my swing in my backyard. Now I'm going to invite my friend who's a golf pro to come and observe my swing and give me feedback. As he's watching, he says, "Whoa, whoa, wait a minute, Mac. Keep your head down. Hold on, keep your left arm straight. Bend those knees." As he gives me this feedback, my swing begins to improve, new habits are developed, and eventually I produce a nice swing that enables me to lower my score by seven strokes. Success!

The focus is on *transformation*, not just the exchange of information. When you practice all three of these elements on a consistent basis, then you see transformation really start to happen.

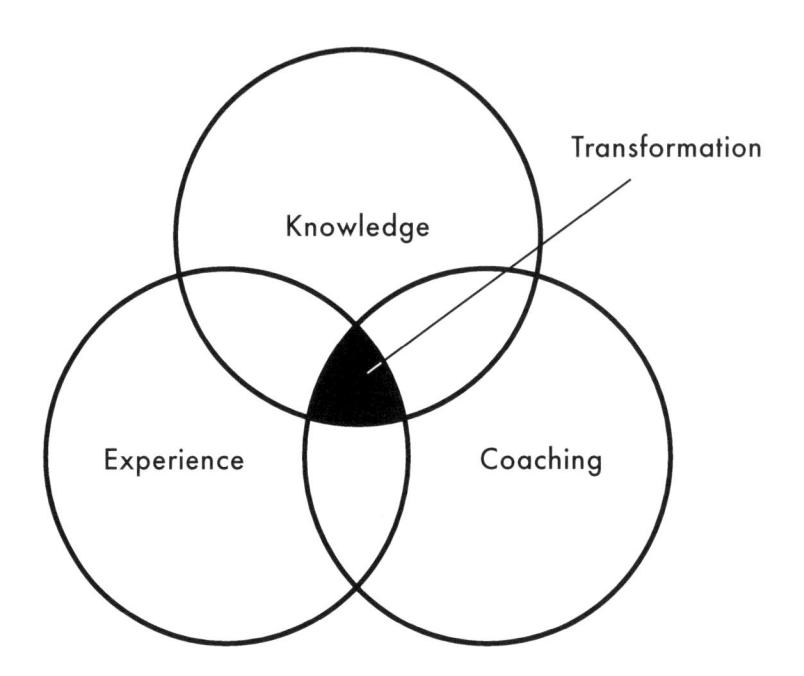

Diagram: Three overlapping circles labeled "Knowledge", "Experience", and "Coaching", with the central intersection labeled "Transformation".

How Do I Get the Most Out of These Modules?

You may have previously participated in leadership training and at the time thought it was really great. Yet a few days later, you're unsure how to apply what you've learned or simply can't remember it. To ensure this is not your experience here, follow these tips:

- Work through the content of the module on your own, making sure you have enough time and headspace to engage with the questions fully. Write your answers and thoughts in the spaces provided throughout the modules.
- Don't just read the "Put It Into Practice" section. Take it seriously and recognize that the practice of the skill is what will help you grow in that area. Take every opportunity to practice what you are learning, whether in your home, work, or church context. This practice will sharpen your skill and build your leadership confidence.

- Every other week, meet with your trainer and up to two other trainees to discuss your reflections. Come to each session ready to share what you learned from the reading and from putting this skill into practice. Your trainer is someone who is experienced at leading others and can give you feedback, insights, and ideas that will better equip you to do the same.
- Shadow your trainer as they lead in their ministry area. Following them around, attending a huddle they are leading, or watching them engage one on one with one of their leaders can be a valuable learning experience as they model healthy leadership to you.

How Long Will the Training Take?

One of the first questions people ask is "How long will it take me to finish this training?" However, the goal is not to "finish" or "get through" the training. The goal is to shape your character and competencies as a leader. Some people will learn and adapt quickly. Others will require more time and practice. Ideally, you can take up to two weeks to complete each module. Meet with your trainer every other week. But don't rush. And don't cram. Pace yourself as a learner to digest the material and put it into practice.

Because *Leading an Organization* is a discipleship-based training rather than a traditional classroom-based training, there is a flexible timeline for you to complete each module. In other words, this mentoring-/discipleship-based approach means you may or may not cover one module in one meeting. You and your trainer may choose to spend several meetings on one topic to ensure you're developing the character and competency for that module. The objective is to demonstrate growth, not just absorb the information.

How Is Each Module Organized?

The modules are very interactive and will require you to write down your answers and reflections. Each module includes various sections that will help you learn more rapidly, including:

- **Learning Objectives**

Focus points to learn as a result of this study. Though you may gain additional learning from the modules, the objectives are designed to guide you to these particular outcomes.

- **Preassessment**

A self-diagnostic to assess your current character and competency before you begin a module.

- **Deepen Your Character**

A study from Scripture on a character trait that undergirds each competency. The study includes questions that help you process the information and spark transformative discussion.

- **Develop Your Competency**

Content about how to develop a particular competency, with follow-up questions.

- **Put It Into Practice**

Assignments to complete and/or review with your trainer.

- **Reflect on Your Learning**

Questions to help you grasp your key takeaways from the module.

Now that you understand the uniqueness of this training and have a big-picture overview, let's dive in and get started.

Overview of Modules

In *Leading an Organization*, you will develop these competencies and grow in these character traits by completing these modules:

Module 1: Perseverance

Character: *Loyalty*
Leaders demonstrate a steadfast dedication to their cause, team, and values, even in the face of adversity.

Competency: *Perseverance*
Unyielding dependence on God that fuels an unrelenting commitment to the mission in the face of difficulties, obstacles, or discouragements.

Module 2: Shaping Culture

Character: *Conviction*
Leaders consistently uphold and act in accordance with a set of core beliefs, regardless of external circumstances.

Competency: *Shaping Culture*
Proactively cultivate and embody the core values that drive a spiritually healthy and productive work environment.

Module 3: Casting Vision

Character: *Submission*
Leaders listen to God's voice, know God's heart, and obediently follow God's will.

Competency: *Casting Vision*
Communicate a clear picture of the future in a way that motivates others to take actions that advance the God-given vision.

Module 4: Teaching

Character: *Confidence*
Leaders fully trust in the guidance of the Holy Spirit, enabling them to approach challenges and decisions with self-assurance and peace.

Competency: *Teaching*
Impart knowledge, skills, and values to learners, inspiring and motivating them to actively engage in personal and spiritual growth.

Module 5: Financial Stewardship

Character: *Generosity*
Leaders manage finances guided by biblical principles, enabling them to participate in God's work of transforming lives and communities.

Competency: *Financial Stewardship*
Implement financial strategies that ensure financial sustainability while maintaining transparency, accountability, and compliance with legal and biblical standards.

Module 6: Leading Change

Character: *Composure*
Leaders consider and honor the perspectives of others, not taking disagreement personally.

Competency: *Leading Change*
Identify the meaningful change that needs to occur in the organization and communicate the changes in a way that honors those involved and brings the majority to embrace the change.

1

Perseverance

Leadership is a journey fraught with challenges, obstacles, and unexpected turns. We all dream of starting strong and finishing well, but the reality is often different. The burdens of guiding an organization can weigh heavily on our souls, eroding our confidence, draining our energy, and even tempting us to surrender. As leaders, it is imperative that we learn to nurture an unwavering reliance on the presence and power of God, enabling us to persevere through the most arduous of times.

I still remember the day I (Mac) heard the news about a pastor I had admired for over twenty years. He had fallen to sexual sin and was removed from leadership. It was a devastating blow, not just for him but also for his family and congregation. How could someone so gifted and inspiring fall so hard? It made me realize how one sinful act can take someone out of leadership and impact the rest of their life.

But moral failure isn't the only factor that can cause leaders to step away from their roles. Unmet expectations, excessive workload, organizational crises, family pressures, critics, and loneliness can also take their toll. These challenges test our resilience, commitment, and faith in profound ways.

We need leaders who can persevere and endure the complex

and painful work of leadership, with an unwavering commitment to God's mission. In Galatians 6:9, Paul reminds us not to become weary in doing good, for at the proper time, we will reap a harvest if we do not give up. The word "weary" in Greek refers to the fatigue a woman experiences in labor. It's a powerful metaphor for the pain and struggle of leadership.

Perseverance is not just about gritting our teeth and pushing through the pain. It's about deepening our dependence on God, seeking his presence and power in every moment.

We define the competency of perseverance as an unyielding dependence on God that fuels an unrelenting commitment to the mission in the face of difficulties, obstacles, or discouragements.

For us, this definition is more than just theoretical. We have personally confronted the pressures and tribulations of organizational leadership at the highest levels. Rick guided Cuyahoga Valley Church (CVC) for a remarkable twenty-six years before entrusting the baton to a successor, yet even at sixty-eight, he remains an integral part of the team, fervently cultivating the development of future leaders. As for me, I (Mac) planted a church, transitioned to a nonprofit, and then, at fifty-nine, started my own business focusing on leadership development. Our diverse experiences and unique perspectives combine to offer you valuable insights that will equip you for your leadership journey.

Without a doubt, every leader will encounter discouragement and fatigue. However, it is how we respond to these challenges that will ultimately define the caliber and longevity of our ministry.

In this session, we will explore the competency of perseverance and its connection to the character trait of loyalty. We will delve into five core issues leaders must continually address to persevere and finish well. We hope our insights and experiences will help you grow in your leadership journey and inspire you to persevere in facing challenges.

First, let's work to define our terms:

Character: *Loyalty*
Leaders demonstrate a steadfast dedication to their cause, team, and values, even in the face of adversity.

Competency: *Perseverance*
Unyielding dependence on God that fuels an unrelenting commitment to the mission in the face of difficulties, obstacles, or discouragements.

Objectives

1. Evaluate your commitment and dedication toward your goals and vision.
2. Develop strategies to rely on God and strengthen your faith in challenging times.
3. Identify and implement practical steps to improve your overall well-being, including physical health.
4. Assess the quality and quantity of your support network and determine areas for improvement.
5. Create and implement clear and effective personal boundaries to protect your emotional and spiritual health.

Deepen your Character: *Loyalty*

Scott Miller, vice president of Thought Leadership for FranklinCovey, shares a story from his early career that illustrates the profound connection between loyalty and perseverance. Upon being promoted to oversee a team of forty highly skilled professionals,

Miller and his family relocated from Salt Lake City to Chicago. Little did he know that a routine visit from a fellow vice president (VP) would serve as a powerful wake-up call.

The VP entered Miller's office and declared an unexpected analogy: "Scott, you are standing at a gas station holding a match." Perplexed and taken aback, Miller listened as the VP proceeded to describe a crucial concern. Since his move to Chicago, Miller had displayed disloyalty through his words and actions toward the VP's leadership. Instances of gossip, breaches of confidence, and disrespect in handling shared information were highlighted.

Deep down, Miller recognized the truth in his boss's words. He acknowledged his failure to act with loyalty and respect, leaving him with a sense of shame and embarrassment. However, this pivotal moment served as a catalyst, impressing upon him a vital lesson about the indispensable value of loyalty in fostering trust and creating a healthy team culture.

From that day onward, Miller made a conscious and deliberate effort to demonstrate unwavering loyalty to his colleagues and leaders. He understood that without loyalty, trust could erode, and the team's morale would suffer. Miller recognized that loyalty was not a mere abstract concept but a foundational character trait that must be exemplified through his daily actions and words.

This intertwining of loyalty and perseverance is evident in the biblical story of Ruth. Despite her Moabite background, Ruth exhibited remarkable loyalty to her mother-in-law, Naomi. Ruth's selfless decision to follow Naomi back to Judah, forsaking her own comfort and security, demonstrated loyalty that defied societal expectations. She declared, "Where you go I will go, and where you stay I will stay. Your people will be my people and your God my

God" (Ruth 1:16–17). Ruth's act of loyalty demanded significant sacrifice but ultimately transformed her life and left an indelible mark on history.

To cultivate and demonstrate loyalty as a leader, consider the following tips:

- **Put your team first**

Prioritize the needs of your team by actively listening, providing support and encouragement, and celebrating their successes. When your team feels valued and appreciated, they are more likely to remain loyal to you and the organization.

- **Lead by example**

As a leader, you set the tone for your organization. Model loyalty through consistency, refraining from speaking negatively about team members, avoiding gossip, following through on commitments, and displaying unwavering dedication to your cause and values.

- **Stay true to your mission**

Loyalty as a leader means remaining steadfast in your commitment to your organization's mission. In the face of challenges, resist the temptation to compromise values or take shortcuts. True loyalty requires staying the course, even when it is difficult, and remaining true to the vision that ignited your leadership journey.

Loyalty serves as a cornerstone for leaders who aspire to build trust and cultivate authentic relationships with those they lead and serve. It intertwines with perseverance, providing the necessary strength and resolve to endure hardships and emerge victorious. By embodying loyalty in your character and actions, you can inspire your team to persevere, thrive, and leave a lasting legacy.

Scripture

As you read the following Scripture, meditate on what the author wishes to communicate, and answer the questions below. Allow the Holy Spirit to speak to you and challenge you as a leader about how you can develop your character so that you are loyal in your everyday life.

Ruth 1:1–18

In the days when the judges ruled, there was a famine in the land. So a man from Bethlehem in Judah, together with his wife and two sons, went to live for a while in the country of Moab. The man's name was Elimelek, his wife's name was Naomi, and the names of his two sons were Mahlon and Kilion. They were Ephrathites from Bethlehem, Judah. And they went to Moab and lived there. Now Elimelek, Naomi's husband, died, and she was left with her two sons. They married Moabite women, one named Orpah and the other Ruth. After they had lived there about ten years, both Mahlon and Kilion also died, and Naomi was left without her two sons and her husband. When Naomi heard in Moab that the Lord had come to the aid of his people by providing food for them, she and her daughters-in-law prepared to return home from there. With her two daughters-in-law she left the place where she had been living and set out on the road that would take them back to the land of Judah. Then Naomi said to her two daughters-in-law, "Go back, each of you, to your mother's home. May the Lord show you kindness, as you have shown kindness to your dead husbands and to me. May the LORD grant that each of you will find rest in the home of another husband." Then she kissed them goodbye and they wept aloud and said to her, "We will go back with you to your people." But Naomi said, "Return home, my daughters. Why would you come with me? Am I going to have any more sons, who could become your husbands? Return home, my daughters; I am too old to have another husband. Even if I thought there was still hope for me—even if I had a husband tonight and then gave birth to sons—would you wait until they grew up? Would you remain unmarried for them? No, my daughters. It is more bitter for me than for you, because the LORD's hand has turned against me!" At this they wept aloud again. Then Orpah kissed her mother-in-law goodbye, but Ruth clung to her. "Look," said Naomi, "your sister-in-law is going back to her people and her gods. Go back with her." But Ruth replied, "Don't urge me to leave you or to turn back from you. Where you go I will go, and where you stay I will stay. Your people will be my people and your God my God. Where you die I will die, and there I will be buried. May the LORD deal with me, be it ever so severely, if even death separates you and me." When Naomi realized that Ruth was determined to go with her, she stopped urging her.

What do you imagine Ruth sacrificed to move to Judah with Naomi? In what way have you sacrificed recently for the sake of your team?

What lessons can be learned from Ruth's story about the power of loyalty in building strong relationships and creating a sense of belonging within a team or community?

In what practical ways can you cultivate loyalty in your team or organization?

Now that we have examined the character trait of loyalty, we can begin to work through the core competency for this module: *perseverance*. *As you read what follows, note how loyalty can undergird a leader's competency in perseverance.*

Develop Your Competency: *Perseverance*
Preassessment

Before proceeding, complete the assessment below. In the final module of this training guide, you will retake it as a postassessment to measure your transformation and growth in this competency.

The following proficiencies demonstrate mastery of this module's competency. For each of them, give yourself a grade of A, B, C, D, or E to reflect your actual level of competency today. Giving yourself an A+ indicates you are a model for others to follow. An E indicates no mastery.

Proficiency	Preassessment
I intentionally cultivate my dependence on God and seek his guidance and strength as I face challenges and obstacles.	
I regularly study and reflect on God's Word—seeking wisdom and guidance to help me persevere through difficult situations.	
I prioritize my relationships with family, friends, and colleagues—recognizing that strong relationships provide support and encouragement when facing challenges.	
I consistently care for my physical and emotional health by eating well, exercising regularly, and getting enough sleep.	
I regularly assess my calling and purpose, seeking to align my goals and actions with God's plan for my life and make adjustments when necessary.	

Which of the five proficiencies do you want to grow in the most? Why is it important for you to grow in that aspect?

Which of the five perseverance proficiencies do you feel strongest in, and why?

> Looking at your overall proficiency assessment, what areas must you focus on to become a more effective and resilient leader? What steps can you take to prioritize those areas and make meaningful progress?

Leading Well ... Finishing Strong

Leading well and finishing strong is the desire of every leader's heart, yet the reality is that many struggle with burnout and discouragement. According to Barna Research, in 2022, 42 percent of pastors considered quitting full-time ministry in the previous twelve months.[1] A 2022 Deloitte study showed that around 70 percent of CEOs and managers are considering quitting their job.[2] These are concerning statistics, highlighting the need for leaders to intentionally cultivate a dependence on God that produces unwavering commitment to their calling.

In the mid-80s, I (Mac) attended a conference where Pastor John Bisagno, the renowned leader of the First Baptist Church of Houston, spoke about a topic close to his heart: the importance of finishing strong in the ministry.

As he shared his insights, Bisagno recounted a story from his college days, when he and over twenty of his closest friends decided to pray for each other throughout their entire ministry journey. Each of them wrote their name on a prayer list in their Bibles, passing it around for everyone to add their own names.

Years passed, and Bisagno often heard of one of his friends dropping out of the ministry for various reasons. Every time he received such news, he would take out his Bible, turn to the front flap where the names were written, and scratch through the name of the fallen friend with a pen.

When Bisagno retired from First Baptist Church Houston, he revisited that same prayer list he had carried for many years. As he flipped through the pages, he realized that out of the original twenty-four names, only three remained: his own and two others.

That realization hit Bisagno hard. These statistics affirmed the importance of perseverance in the face of adversity. His story is a powerful reminder that while starting strong is important, finishing strong is what matters.

Rick and I have seen similar experiences in our ministry journeys. It's clear that starting strong is easy but, for all of us, finishing strong takes intentionality and intimacy in our relationship with Jesus. As Jesus said in Matthew 11:28–30, "Come to me, all you who are weary and burdened, and I will give you rest. Take my yoke upon you and learn from me, for I am gentle and humble in heart, and you will find rest for your souls. For my yoke is easy and my burden is light." We have to learn not to carry everything on our shoulders but to give everything to him.

In this session, we will give you six habits that enable leaders to persevere through difficulty. By focusing on these habits, you can build the resilience and endurance needed to lead well and finish strong.

Habit #1: Cultivate a Dependence on the Holy Spirit

It's Monday morning, and things aren't going well. You're discouraged because your organization's outreach efforts haven't yielded the desired results, financial support is declining, and you've consistently faced challenges during important meetings. Balancing your responsibilities has taken a toll on your personal relationships, leaving you feeling overwhelmed, defeated, and disconnected. This recurring feeling has become a familiar part of your Mondays.

You want to give up, but you won't. You're not a quitter. However, it's essential to ask yourself, "Am I seeking to persevere in the flesh or the Spirit?"

Persevering in a self-reliant way will lead to frustration, anger, resentment, bitterness, burnout, or moral failure. In contrast, persevering in the Spirit will lead to love, joy, and peace.

You are gifted, creative, innovative, and adaptive. But remind yourself that your best human effort means nothing apart from the energizing life of Jesus flowing in and through you.

Jesus said, "I am the vine; you are the branches. If you remain in me and I in you, you will bear much fruit; apart from me you can do nothing" (John 15:5).

Persevering is the fruit of remaining. Seeking to persevere in organizational leadership while not abiding in Christ is the same as persisting in our own strength. Pressing on through self-effort is fruitless, and it is like "chasing after the wind" (Ecclesiastes 1:14). It is dead works and "running … in vain" (Galatians 2:2), "labor[ing] in vain" (Philippians 2:16), and is building a foundation on "wood, hay or straw" (1 Corinthians 3:12).

Toughing it out when we're not abiding in Christ may seem like success in the eyes of men, but it's not a win in God's eyes. Moreover, this so-called "success" may reinforce even more self-effort on our part.

Therefore, we should pray, "O God, save us from 'successful' self-effort." Unless we persevere in a God-dependent way, all we have produced is wood, hay, and straw.

In his book *Secrets of the Vine*, Bruce Wilkinson gives an insight into the nature of abiding. He writes:

> Picture the place where ancient trunk meets vigorous branch. Here is the touchpoint, the place where abiding happens. Here is the connection where life-giving nutrients in the sap flow through to the developing fruit. The only limitation on the amount of sap that goes to the fruit is the circumference of the branch where it meets the vine. That means that the branch with the largest, least-obstructed connection with the vine is abiding the most and will have the greatest potential for a huge crop.[3]

To yield true spiritual fruit, we must stay connected to Jesus widely, constantly, deeply, and purely. As leaders, we are often tempted to doubt and even disbelieve what Jesus is saying in John 15:5. We may see other leaders who don't claim to be Christian but seem to be accomplishing a lot of good. However, even though human effort apart from Christ can sometimes give the appearance of vibrant life, over time, self-reliance becomes unsustainable. That's when we crash.

How passionate are you about living in utter dependence on God to persist in your kingdom work? In 2 Chronicles, King Jehoshaphat prayed to God when an overpowering army surrounded his kingdom, "We do not know what to do, but our eyes are on you" (2 Chronicles 20:12). Are you totally dependent on God like that? 24/7/365? Really? Some of us trust God, but only with 10, 20, 50, or 90 percent of the problem.

Maybe you're exhausted because you've been trusting too much in your own ingenuity to keep going. Or perhaps things are just ... common and boring. There's no sense of the supernatural. Or perhaps you've been coming up with the best plans, strategies, and effort to hang tough. You've been implementing good advice from family and friends. You've read the right books. But you honestly have to admit that toughing it out has become dutiful drudgery. You lack the joy of the Lord.

To persevere in our calling, we must fully rely on Jesus. Human effort alone will eventually fail. We need to surrender ourselves completely, trusting him 24/7/365. By embracing our dependence on God, we tap into his supernatural strength and find joy. We need to let go of self-reliance, fix our gaze on Jesus, and cultivate a dependence on the Holy Spirit. In him, we discover the unwavering perseverance and abundant life we seek.

> *In what ways have you been tempted to rely on your own strength and abilities instead of depending on the Holy Spirit in your life and ministry?*

What must you do to intentionally cultivate a deeper relationship with God and abide in him to avoid burnout and failure?

Habit #2: Establish a Christ-Centered Identity

The Apostle Paul summarized his life with these words: "I consider my life worth nothing to me; my only aim is to finish the race and complete the task the Lord Jesus has given me—the task of testifying to the good news of God's grace" (Acts 20:24). However, sometimes we lose sight of our mission and become discouraged in our pursuit. When this happens, we start to question our calling and prioritize our success over our commitment to persevere in what God has called us to be and do.

I (Rick) was in a similar situation when I planted CVC. We were stuck at the two hundred barrier—a common attendance number many church planters struggle to surpass. Our attendance fluctuated, and we plateaued. At that point, I began questioning my calling and looking for other ministry opportunities. Perseverance wasn't a priority for me.

I didn't realize my problem until a friend helped me see that my temptation to give up was rooted in my insecurity. I had not yet learned to serve out of my identity in Christ. I was basing my worth on whether our attendance was always growing. I was obsessed with success but didn't realize that my present drive was rooted in my past pain.

As a young man, I always loved baseball and dreamed of making it to the major leagues. I played baseball in college at Vanderbilt University and was drafted by the Minnesota Twins after college. I spent five years in the minor leagues but never made it to the majors. My identity took a hit because I felt I had failed as a ballplayer, and I brought that baggage into the ministry. I thought, *If I can't be "major league" in baseball, then I will be "major league" as a pastor instead.* But when the attendance at CVC stopped climbing, I felt I wasn't what a "major league" pastor should be, so I concluded it was time to move on.

I didn't realize I was using ministry to shore up my shaky self-esteem. I was driving myself to succeed to validate my existence, but my commitment to persevere plummeted when I did not hit the marks I set for myself.

To be a spiritual leader that perseveres, you must find your identity in Christ. You must understand any broken motivations in your heart and unpack your bad baggage. You must learn to become increasingly secure in God's love.

The late Christian counselor and author Larry Crabb asked, "Do you have an exclamation point or a question mark in your heart?"[4] We are all born with a question mark in our hearts, wondering whether we have worth, value, and love. When people with a question-marked heart go into ministry, they can cause great damage to others. They develop visions, goals, strategies, and tactics for ministry and then use people to answer the questions, "Am I loved? Do I matter?"

On the other hand, exclamation-pointed people are secure in their identity in Christ. They know they are loved and have worth and value. They develop visions, goals, strategies, and tactics for ministry, but they don't use people; they serve them. Exclamation-pointed people leave a good and godly legacy, and the people they lead feel served rather than used.

Are you serving with a deep, abiding confidence that God loves you? Perseverance in ministry is supercharged when our question-marked heart is transformed into an exclamation-pointed heart.

Remember how Jesus started his ministry? He was baptized, and the Father's voice from heaven announced, "This is my Son, whom I love; with him I am well pleased" (Matthew 3:17). As Jesus launched his public ministry, the Father knew it was vital for Jesus in his humanity to know how much the Father loved him. Rejection, accusations, ridicule, and suffering were coming. Despite an apparent lack of success, Jesus didn't quit. The Father's love enabled him to set his "face like flint" (Isaiah 50:7).

The knowledge of being loved by God was foundational for Jesus in his ministry. If that was true for Jesus, how much more must it be true for us?

You are his "handiwork, created in Christ Jesus to do good works, which God prepared in advance for [you] to do" (Ephesians 2:10). When we understand our identity in Christ, we are free to pursue the good works he has prepared for us without the pressure to perform or earn our worth. As we serve out of a sense of security in God's love, we can persevere in our calling, even when faced with challenges and setbacks. Our Christ-centered identity gives us the foundation to run the race with endurance, knowing that our ultimate value and worth come from our relationship with Christ, not our ministry success.

> Think of a leader you know who is secure in God's love. How did that leader grow to be so secure?

Habit #3: Prioritize Physical Health

Every day, between four or five in the afternoon, I (Mac) would come home from a long day of pastoring and lay on the couch. Inevitably, just as I was dozing off for a much-needed nap, one or all three of my young children would interrupt me, wanting me to play. Getting up from that couch felt like lifting a 240-pound sack of potatoes from the ground. At age forty, I told Cindy, my wife, "I'm still young but feel so old." I was tired, overweight, and living with a high-stress level.

Then one day, I stumbled upon a verse in Deuteronomy that would change my life forever: "Moses was a hundred and twenty years old when he died, yet his eyes were not weak nor his strength gone" (Deuteronomy 34:7). I was struck by the fact that when God retired Moses from ministry, it wasn't because he was tired and worn out; it was because he had completed his life mission. He lived the later years of his life with full vitality and energy.

Inspired by this, I decided to embark on a grand experiment. Rather than trying a diet, I would change my lifestyle. For the next three months, I started eating healthy, exercising, and taking time off from work. The results were remarkable. As I gave up soft drinks, fried foods, and sugary snacks, I lost forty pounds and gained energy. But more than that, my joy returned, and my "light depression" subsided. I discovered that my physical disciplines impacted not just my physical health but my spiritual health as well. How I feel physically influences how I feel spiritually.

This experience led Cindy and me to a new life goal: "We want to die young at an old age." Moses gave me an example of what it might be like to live the full extent of my life with vitality and energy.

But as a leader of an organization, I know that prioritizing physical health is easier said than done. The demands of leadership can be overwhelming, and it's easy to neglect self-care while caring for others. I also know that if I don't take care of myself, I won't be able to care for others effectively.

I had received this advice years earlier but had neglected it. When I was in seminary, I remember Dr. Howard Hendricks asked our seminary class, "Do you want me to tell you how to add fifteen more years to your ministry?" I grabbed my pen and awaited the spiritual secret. To my surprise, he said, "Eat right, and exercise every day."

It took me many years, but I finally realized he was right. Taking care of my physical health wasn't just about feeling better in the short term. It was about being able to serve God and others for the long haul.

So, I started prioritizing four essentials to increase my energy levels and maintain my physical health: eat, sleep, move, and think.

■ Eat

Food is fuel. It converts into energy that enables us to move and feel good. However, not all food is good fuel. Some foods rob you of energy and harm your overall health. Much of the food in the US today is processed and contains chemicals and other elements our bodies struggle to process. As a result, many people suffer from heart disease, obesity, hypertension, and depression. Changing what you eat can change your mood, energy, and health.

- **Sleep**

I used to think that sleeping less meant accomplishing more. But as I learned more about sleep, I realized that's far from the truth. Quality sleep is essential to your physical, emotional, and mental health and your productivity. It's not about how many hours you spend in bed; it's about how many hours of quality sleep you get.

If you struggle with getting quality sleep, please check out one of my favorite books, *Sleep Smarter* by Shawn Stevenson.[5] He provides twenty-one strategies to help achieve high-quality sleep. One of the most practical tips is to create a sleep routine—set a bedtime and a wake-up time and stick to it. Our bodies thrive on routine, and creating a consistent sleep schedule can help you sleep better and feel more refreshed.

- **Move**

Leading an organization can be demanding, and it's easy to find yourself sitting behind a computer or in meetings all day long. Movement is essential to maintain muscle, bone, joint, brain, lung, and heart health. It's too important to ignore, so schedule movement into your daily calendar. Find an exercise routine that works for you, whether it's walking, your favorite sport, or weightlifting. One simple tip anyone can apply is to take walks during your phone calls, even if it is simply doing laps around the office space. Every little movement matters.

- **Think**

Leading an organization can be stressful, damaging your health in numerous ways. A 2021 Lifeway study reported that 63 percent of the pastors surveyed said they "frequently" feel overwhelmed. According to the survey, the top things that stress pastors out are "church conflict, the feeling of being on-call 24/7 and other unrealistic expectations and a general sense of isolation."[6]

It's crucial to take time to care for your mental health. Find activities that bring you joy and relaxation—whether reading, listening to music, or spending time in nature. Consider talking to a therapist or counselor to process your emotions and manage stress.

As leaders, we are called to be good stewards of all God has given us, including our physical and mental health. We cannot fulfill our mission if we are tired, stressed, and unhealthy. Prioritizing our health can be challenging, but it's worth it.

> How would you assess the condition of your physical health? Unhealthy, Average Health, or Very Healthy?

Which of the four areas is your strongest: Eat, Sleep, Move, or Think? Weakest?

What next step do you need to take to improve your physical health?

Habit #4: Maintain God's Perspective on Your Problems

As a rookie church planter, I (Mac) had grand plans to grow our congregation and reach our community. But I didn't realize God had a plan for me that involved using the church to grow me.

Things were looking up at the start of the journey. We launched our church plant in a new elementary school and had 307 people attend our opening Sunday. But just three weeks later, our world came crashing down when the school board delivered a devastating blow—we had to vacate the premises within three months unless we proved we had purchased a property or had architectural drawings for a new building. The school board members were concerned because another church plant in the area was using a different school and had been in that facility for seven years. Not wanting our church to be a long-term tenant, they put these requirements on us to ensure we would be out of the school within a year or two. And to make things worse there were no alternative sites in the community we could rent.

At that moment, I felt helpless and defeated. How could we possibly accomplish all of that in just three months? Was this the end of our church-planting journey? I questioned God's calling and feared the worst.

The next three months were a grueling test of our faith as we prayed and trusted God's plan. Miraculously, a generous donor stepped forward and helped us purchase twenty-five acres of land only one mile from the school. And just as quickly, an architect put together some affordable plans that allowed us to stay in the school until our building was ready three years later.

Looking back on that trying time, I realize that the growth I experienced during those early years as a church planter came not from my own wisdom or brilliance but from the challenges, obstacles, and discouragement I and the whole congregation faced together. And I wouldn't have it any other way! It was through those struggles that God grew my ability to look for his perspective in challenging times.

That experience did two things. First, it tested my commitment to the vision. Circumstances would have made it easy to conclude we were not supposed to plant this church. The episode pushed and deepened my conviction that God had called us to plant this church. Second, it showed me the faithfulness of God. It's when things look impossible, God can and does still work.

When you lead an organization, you will face circumstances that test your faith and resolve. There will be times you will want to quit. But leaders who develop the ability to see God's perspective will persevere through the tough times.

In the face of difficulty, the question is not, "How do I get out of this?" The question is, "God, how do you want me to go through this?" The question is not, "Should I quit?" The question is, "God, what is my next step?"

I've coached many pastors, telling them, "Your problem isn't your problem; your perspective is your problem." When we lose perspective on the faithfulness and power of God, it's easy to give up when circumstances look impossible.

Whenever you are feeling discouraged and tempted to give up, ask yourself these questions:

- What is God trying to teach me (and our organization)?
- What "impossible" request is God asking me to trust him for?
- What lie am I tempted to believe during this challenge?
- What truth from God's Word must I embrace during this challenge?

Praying through these questions will help you regain God's perspective on your situation.

Habit #5: Foster a Supportive Community

As leaders, we may sometimes feel pressure to maintain a professional facade that can take a toll on our mental and emotional well-being. This is especially true for leaders, who may become trapped behind a glittering image, cut off from God and their true selves. In some cases, this can lead to depression and even suicide.

To avoid such outcomes, we must prioritize our own spiritual growth and emotional health, seeking genuine community and practicing the "one another" commands of the New Testament.[7] As leaders, we must remember we are not above our people and we, too, need to be transformed into the image of Christ.

One powerful way to achieve this transformation is through authentic relationships with other leaders who can provide encouragement, accountability, and support. While it's possible to develop these relationships within your organization, we have found it helpful to seek out connections with leaders outside of the local context, where it is safe to be vulnerable and acknowledge our struggles.

Unfortunately, ministry leaders often view each other as competitors rather than brothers and sisters who can build each other up. We need to shift our thinking and recognize that leaders of organizations are disciples in need of the same grace we teach to those we serve. By surrounding ourselves with trusted friends, advisors, mentors, and coaches committed to our well-being, we can deal with the challenges and limitations of ministry and finish strong.

I (Rick) have been blessed to have such relationships in my life, including a twice-monthly pastor's forum I've been part of for over twenty-five years. We don't focus on ministry strategy or "talk shop," but rather, we talk about our hearts, relationships, and attitudes. I've also relied on trusted counselors whenever I've faced emotional or relational challenges. This has helped me weather some extremely difficult storms.

In short, as we strive to persevere and finish strong as leaders, let's not neglect the importance of genuine community and supportive relationships. By prioritizing our spiritual and emotional health and seeking out trusted allies, we can avoid the pitfalls of burnout and depression and instead fulfill our calling with joy and effectiveness.

Habit #6: Set Clear Boundaries

Many leaders struggle to finish strong because they fail to establish healthy boundaries that keep them spiritually, relationally, emotionally, and physically healthy. Here are some boundaries to consider as you strive to protect your soul:

- **Family boundaries**

Your first ministry is to your family. If your home life is not in order, it can quickly drain your emotional and spiritual reserves, leaving you ill-equipped to lead effectively. To avoid this, you must establish healthy boundaries, prioritizing quality time with your spouse and children. This can include taking regular days off, scheduling family vacations, and planning date nights. By investing in your family relationships, you protect them and ensure you have the support you need to thrive in your leadership role.

- **Structure boundaries**

As a CEO or senior pastor, it is essential to acknowledge the limits of your leadership capacity. Although trying to lead everyone directly may be tempting, this approach is only sustainable in the short run. Instead, you need to establish a well-defined organizational structure that limits the number of direct reports you have. As Jethro warned Moses in Exodus 18, trying to handle everything alone will lead to burnout. By delegating responsibility and building a structure that provides leadership and care for everyone in your organization, you can avoid this pitfall and ensure you finish strong.

- **Time boundaries**

Leaders are often visionaries, driven to accomplish great things in a short amount of time. Although this can be admirable, it can lead to overcommitment and burnout. You must establish time boundaries to manage your schedule effectively to avoid this. This can involve saying no more often, prioritizing your time, and recognizing that some things take longer than expected. Doing so can help you avoid overextending yourself and ensure you have the time and energy to pursue your goals and priorities.

- **Relationship boundaries**

As a leader, you are called to serve and love others, but it is also crucial to recognize that some relationships can drain your energy and resources. To maintain your spiritual and emotional well-being, it is essential to establish healthy boundaries with people who have a negative impact on you. This may involve taking breaks from certain individuals or seeking support from trusted friends or mentors. Like Jesus, who withdrew to be alone after periods of intense ministry, establishing healthy rhythms that allow you to refuel your soul is essential to finishing strong.

By establishing boundaries around family, structure, time, and relationships, you can protect your spiritual, relational, emotional, and physical well-being, ensuring you have a healthy walk with God and everything you need to lead effectively over the long term.

> Which of these boundary areas do you struggle with the most? What next steps do you need to take to strengthen that boundary? Who can you discuss this with to help you or hold you accountable?

Conclusion

Although this module has focused on perseverance, there are times when it is appropriate to transition out of your role. Even when you're loyal to your calling, leaving for a new assignment is possible. When questioning and praying about a potential transition, ask yourself:

- Am I running away from something, or am I running toward something?
- Have I lost my passion for what I do? Is it temporary or permanent?
- Will the new assignment stretch my faith, or am I taking the easy route?
- Has the calling been affirmed by godly people and is it aligned with my gifts and passion?
- If married, is my spouse in favor of the potential transition?

Ultimately, maintaining healthy boundaries and persevering through challenges requires wisdom, discernment, and a willingness to adapt as necessary. By prioritizing your well-being and seeking God's guidance, you can stay committed to your calling while maintaining a fruitful and fulfilling ministry.

> **Put It Into Practice**
>
> Developing a new skill requires practice. Before you get together with your trainer, complete some of the following assignments to help you practice perseverance.
>
> 1. Identify a problem in your area of leadership and assess your attitude toward the issue. Spend extended time in prayer regarding that challenge. Journal your thoughts and insights on the character of God and your own character during this season. Consider how you can rely more fully on God's strength and wisdom as you persevere. Then brainstorm a list of solutions to overcome this challenge and commit to implementing one of the solutions. Meet with your trainer to discuss your progress and receive feedback on your perseverance.

2. Coach a leader whose morale seems low due to a challenge and help them develop a healthy perspective. This will require patience, empathy, and a willingness to invest time and energy in someone else's growth.

3. Search for Scripture passages about perseverance, and write them in a journal. Write a one-page journal entry, expressing what God impresses on your heart about this competency. Meditate on these verses regularly and ask God to give you the strength to persevere through difficulties.

4. Research how other leaders have persevered through difficult situations. Google "How successful Christian leaders persevere" and write a summary of what you learned. Use these insights to inform your own approach to perseverance.

5. Interview a leader with a long tenure in their role, and ask them what they have learned about perseverance. Journal your insights from the conversation and share them with your trainer.

Reflect on Your Learning

Where did you grow the most in this competency?

What next step do you need to take to continue to grow in this competency?

Meet With Your Trainer

Consistent practice can be a great beginning to sharpening a skill, but developing a skill also requires processing what you learned with others.

Meet with your trainer and discuss what you learned from this module.

Dig Deeper

If you are leading or participating in an internship or want to continue to grow in the competency of perseverance, go to https://www.multiplygroup.org/internship-planner to download the companion guide to this book.

---

[1] Tish Harrison Warren, "Why Pastors Are Burning Out," *The New York Times*, August 28, 2022, https://www.nytimes.com/2022/08/28/opinion/pastor-burnout-pandemic.html#.

[2] Jack Kelly, "CEOs Are Quitting And Joining The Great Resignation—Here's Why," *Forbes*, June 29, 2022, https://www.forbes.com/sites/jackkelly/2022/06/29/ceos-are-quitting-and-joining-the-great-resignation-heres-why/?sh=3d1e8a223031.

[3] Bruce Wilkinson, *Secrets of the Vine: Breaking Through to Abundance* (Colorado Springs, CO: Multnomah Books, 2002), 95.

[4] I (Rick) heard Crabb ask this question at a pastors conference in Cleveland in the early 2000s.

[5] Shawn Stevenson, *Sleep Smarter: 21 Essential Strategies to Sleep Your Way to A Better Body, Better Health, and Bigger Success* (New York, NY: Rodale Books, 2016).

[6] "Surprise, Surprise: Research Says Pastors Are Getting More Stressed," *Relevant*, October 27, 2021, https://relevantmagazine.com/culture/surprise-surprise-research-says-pastors-are-getting-more-stressed/#.

[7] See the full list at Andrew Mason, "The 59 One Anothers of the Bible," Small Group Churches, accessed September 8, 2023, https://www.smallgroupchurches.com/the-59-one-anothers-of-the-bible/.

2

Shaping Culture

As a leader, you hold a powerful responsibility for shaping your organization's culture. It cannot be overstated how crucial a healthy culture is to accomplishing your vision.

But what is culture? Organizational culture refers to the shared patterns of behavior and attitudes among a team, which shape people's experience with your organization.

It was 2001, and I (Mac) was attending a John Maxwell leadership conference that would forever alter my perspective on shaping organizational culture. As I sat among my peers, Maxwell shared a simple yet profound statement that would resonate with me for years to come: "If you've been leading your organization for more than three years, then every problem in your organizational culture is a reflection of your leadership."

At the time, I had been leading the Carolina Forest Community Church for four years, and I couldn't help but reflect on the challenges that plagued our operations. Communication was poor, and our team lacked the discipline to execute projects well. As Maxwell's words echoed in my mind, I began to realize that these issues were a reflection of my own leadership style.

It was a sobering realization, and I knew that if our culture was going to change, then I had to change first. I began to take a hard look at how I led the church and the impact it was having on our team. Although it was difficult, I took responsibility for initiating changes.

The transformation wasn't easy, but it was worth it. Over time, we developed a healthy and thriving culture that propelled us toward God's vision. And looking back, Maxwell's words were absolutely true—the culture of the organization is a reflection of the leader.

As the primary leader of an organization, you are the chief culture officer. You cannot delegate or leave the responsibility of shaping the culture to chance. Every organization has a culture, and it's one you've either intentionally shaped or unintentionally allowed.

When you don't know how to shape culture, rest assured there are other factors that will shape it, such as:

- the person with the loudest voice
- the individual with the most influence
- a crisis that you don't take hold of
- unhealthy or poor habits of key leaders in the organization
- poor leadership that doesn't clarify expectations or provide accountability

All of these can contribute to a culture people don't enjoy being a part of.

Therefore, it is essential for leaders to actively shape their organization's culture to enable effective change and drive success. A study by Deloitte found that 82 percent of CEOs believe that culture is a potential competitive advantage, yet only a small percentage feel that their company's culture is where it needs to be.[1] This highlights the need for leaders to prioritize building a healthy culture.

A healthy culture can help drive motivation, productivity, and spiritual growth, leading to deeper team member engagement. On the other hand, a toxic or dysfunctional culture can cause turnover, low morale, and decreased productivity, ultimately negatively impacting progress toward God's mission for the organization.

As you embark on this journey to build a healthy culture in your organization, it's important to remember that change starts with you. In the following sections, we will explore key strategies that can help you shape your organization's culture and drive success.

First, let's work to define the character and competency that shape a healthy culture.

Character: *Conviction*
Leaders consistently uphold and act in accordance with a set of core beliefs, regardless of external circumstances.

Competency: *Shaping Culture*
Proactively cultivate and embody the core values that drive a spiritually healthy and productive work environment.

Objectives

1. Reflect on your personal commitment to your organization's values and assess the degree of conviction you have around each.
2. Practice articulating your organization's core values clearly and concisely.
3. Develop a plan for effectively communicating your organization's values to your team through various channels.
4. Regularly evaluate how well you and your team are living up to the organization's values, and identify areas for improvement.
5. Explore strategies to increase your team's engagement and commitment to the organization's mission and values.

Deepen Your Character:
Conviction

Have you ever met someone who just exudes leadership? Someone who, when they speak, commands your attention and inspires you to action. That's how I (Mac) felt when I first met George Greene, the founder and CEO of Water Missions International (WMI).

WMI is a nonprofit that's on a mission to bring safe drinking water to undeveloped regions of the world and end the global water crisis. George may not look like the typical global leader—he's not large in stature and not particularly eloquent—but because of his enthusiasm and passion you can't help but listen when he speaks.

During our first meeting, George shared with me the history of WMI and his vision for the future. He told me about the two billion people on the planet who don't have access to clean water and how 2,300 people die every day from waterborne diseases. His passion and conviction for this cause were so strong that I couldn't say no when he and his wife, Molly, invited me to join the effort.

Over the next several years, I had the opportunity to travel with George and Molly as they worked tirelessly to provide water for every village in Honduras. I've never seen a couple work so passionately and with such conviction. It was truly contagious.

And that's the thing about conviction—it inspires others to act. Effective leadership requires conviction. It keeps you committed to your mission, and it demands a higher standard of attitudes and actions from your team. It gives you the courage to hold people accountable for their actions.

Think about it—when you know someone truly has conviction, you can feel it. You know they stand for something, and they're not going to waver. But when someone lacks conviction, it's equally apparent.

This isn't just true in the business world; it's true in every aspect of life. Even Jesus demonstrated this when he first began his public ministry. He started out low-key, but then he returned to Jerusalem for the first Passover since starting his ministry, and he made a bold move. He walked into the temple courts and saw the money changers and merchants turning a place of worship into a marketplace. And he did something about it. He made a whip, drove the animals out of the temple, and turned over the money changers' tables (John 2:13–17). That's conviction.

So, if you're a leader—whether in a business, church, or nonprofit—remember the power of conviction. People will follow you when they know you stand for something and you're not afraid to act.

Scripture

As you read the following Scripture, meditate on what the author wishes to communicate and answer the questions below. Allow the Holy Spirit to speak to you and challenge you as a leader about how you can develop your character so that you have a growing sense of conviction in your everyday life.

John 2:13-17

When it was almost time for the Jewish Passover, Jesus went up to Jerusalem. In the temple courts he found people selling cattle, sheep and doves, and others sitting at tables exchanging money. So he made a whip out of cords, and drove all from the temple courts, both sheep and cattle; he scattered the coins of the money changers and overturned their tables. To those who sold doves he said, "Get these out of here! Stop turning my Father's house into a market!" His disciples remembered that it is written: "Zeal for your house will consume me."

If you were one of Jesus' followers at this time, what would be going through your mind as you watched Jesus take this stand in the temple?

Jesus is still in his first year of public ministry at this point. What were some of the potential consequences you might expect as a result of Jesus' actions? Why do you think it was important Jesus took this stand at the beginning of his public ministry?

Think of a leader you know who demonstrates deep conviction. How is that conviction demonstrated in their leadership actions?

Where do you demonstrate conviction? Where do you need to demonstrate greater levels of conviction?

Now that we have examined the character trait of conviction, we can begin working through the core competency for this module: *shaping culture*. As you read what follows, note how conviction can undergird a leader's competency in shaping an organization's culture.

Develop Your Competency: *Shaping Culture*
Preassessment

Before proceeding, complete the assessment below. In the final module of this training guide, you will retake it as a postassessment to measure your transformation and growth in this competency.

The following proficiencies demonstrate mastery of this module's competency. For each of them, give yourself a grade of A, B, C, D, or E to reflect your actual level of competency today. Giving yourself an A+ indicates you are a model for others to follow. An E indicates no mastery.

Proficiency	Preassessment
I have a strong sense of conviction around each one of our organizational values.	
I prioritize open and ongoing communication with our team about our organizational values, regularly discussing how they inform our actions and decisions.	
I lead by example and intentionally model our organizational values in my own behavior, serving as a positive role model for others.	
I regularly evaluate the health and effectiveness of our organizational culture, working collaboratively with my team to identify areas of strength and areas for improvement.	
I use our organizational values to guide decisions, ensuring every action and choice aligns with our shared principles and priorities.	

Which of the five proficiencies do you want to grow in the most? Why is it important for you to grow in that aspect?

Which of the values of your organization do you live out the best? The least? What steps do you need to take to live out the values more consistently?

Shaping the Organizational Culture

I (Mac) am a people person. I thrive on collaboration and teamwork and envisioning a bright future with others. During my time in seminary, I took a part-time job at a data collection company and was excited for the opportunity to work with others and make a decent hourly wage to support my family as I pursued my education. But when I arrived at work each day, I was met with a culture that couldn't have been further from what I hoped for. I was relegated to a small cubicle, given a set of cold-call assignments, and expected to call strangers I would never talk to again. Neither my boss nor anyone from the team ever took the time to get to know me or even ask for my opinion on improving things. It seemed like they just wanted me to come in and do my job like a robot.

Before long, I began to dread going to work. I found myself giving the bare minimum. The unhealthy culture caused by uptight, stressed-out managers was contagious, and it flowed down to the rest of the team. I was disengaged and distant and couldn't bring myself to give my best effort.

When leading an organization, it can be easy to blame individuals on our team for being disengaged or distant. But before pointing fingers, we need to consider what is causing them to disengage.

We believe disengagement stems from one of two factors:

Factor #1: An Unhealthy Culture
A toxic work culture can manifest in many ways: favoritism, unhealthy competition, gossip, an expectation of high results without providing the support or resources to do so, and negative or critical attitudes. These traits create a culture that destroys trust, authenticity, and collaboration. When people sense the culture is unhealthy, they begin to disengage and refrain from bringing their best.

Factor #2: Misaligned Values
On the other hand, some people disengage from work because the culture doesn't align with their values. They simply aren't a good fit for the organization, and that's okay. This is why we must spend extensive time getting to know someone's values before hiring them to ensure good alignment with our organization. They may have the necessary skills for the job, but without values alignment, they won't stick around long.

Here's an example to better illustrate the importance of values alignment in an organization. Imagine two glass bowls, one filled with water and the other with sand. In the water bowl is a fish, and in the sand-filled bowl is a lizard. Both animals are perfectly adapted to their respective environments and therefore thrive. However, if they were to be swapped around and the fish was placed in the sand-filled bowl and the lizard in the water, both animals would struggle to survive.

The culture you create is the environment your team lives in day in and day out. And someone might struggle in a work environment if their values don't align with the organization's values. It's not that one person is right and the other is wrong; they just have different values. Or to put it another way, they may function better in a different environment.

To understand an organization's culture, you only need to observe the top leaders over thirty days. You can discover their values by watching how they treat their employees, respond to crises, and how they spend their money and time. You can see the values by what excites them or makes them angry.

Some cultures are fast, and others are slow. Some are decisive, while others require lengthy processing to make decisions. Some are passive, while others are aggressive. Some cultures focus on relationships, while others focus more on results.

As leaders, it's crucial to keep a close eye on our organization's culture and how it affects our team. When our team's values align with the organization's, you'll notice team members are more engaged. They'll build strong bonds with their teammates, feel a real sense of togetherness, and they'll stick around because they've found a place where they fit right in. Our goal should always be to create a culture where people aren't just surviving but thriving.

Shaping a Healthy Organizational Culture

Now let's consider five keys to shaping a healthy organizational culture.

Key #1: Clarity—Define Your Core Values

To shape the culture of your organization or church, the first step is to define your core values. Consistently living out these values over time will allow you to shape the culture you desire. To do this, it's best to collaborate with your team and identify the traits that currently define your organization. Then, create a list of the traits you aspire to embody. From these lists, choose your top five core values that reflect who you are as an organization.

It's important to use specific and easily understandable language when wording your core values. You can use one of three approaches: a single word, a catchy phrase, or an actionable statement.

- **Approach #1: The single word**

Sometimes, a single word can encapsulate a core value, such as *passion*, *generosity*, or *excellence*. The benefit of this approach is that it's simple to remember. However, it may lack the necessary detail to fully convey the meaning behind the value.

- **Approach #2: The catchphrase**

A catchy and memorable phrase, such as "No one walks alone" or "Saved people save people," can also capture a core value. However, it may not be immediately understandable or measurable.

- **Approach #3: The actionable statement**

An actionable statement is a full sentence or phrase focusing on observable behavior, such as "Make bold moves" or "Collaborate for kingdom impact." This approach is easy to understand, but may be more difficult to remember.

When deciding which approach to use, consider which is most intuitive and realistic for you and your team. By clearly defining your core values through one of these approaches, you can set a strong foundation for shaping your organization's culture.

Key #2: Communication—Share the Values

Defining your values is just the first step. You need to communicate those values effectively to shape culture. However, communicating your values is not a one-time event.

Most churches and organizations share their core values during onboarding, orientation, or hiring. This is a good start, but communicating values is an ongoing practice that should happen daily and week-to-week. Your culture always evolves, and new people coming in or leaving can affect it.

Paul experienced this as he encountered people whose behaviors didn't align with his values and ultimately harmed the mission. He wrote to Timothy, "Do your best to come to me quickly, for Demas, because he loved this world, has deserted me and has gone to Thessalonica" (2 Timothy 4:9–10).

Paul faced the reality that not everyone on his team aligned with the values he established. Many leaders today encounter the same thing. So it's important to communicate your values clearly and consistently.

There are three ways to communicate values effectively and shape your culture:

- **Visibility**

Your core values should guide how your organization operates, clarify decision-making, and engage your team. However, many leaders only push the vision and neglect to engrain the values that will help the team behave in ways that help the vision become a reality.

Ensuring that your team understands and embraces your organization's core values is crucial for effective leadership. Your values should serve as a compass, guiding your organization's operations, clarifying decision-making processes, and engaging your team members. Unfortunately, many leaders focus solely on promoting their vision while neglecting to embed the values that are essential for translating that vision into reality.

I (Mac) have seen Columbia International University (CIU) live out its strong core values firsthand. I've had the privilege of meeting their former president, Dr. Bill Jones, and several CIU staff. Their commitment to Scripture and world missions shines through in everything they do and say. When I finally had the opportunity to visit the campus, I began to understand why their values were so visible in their lives. On the campus grounds, they have CIU's five core values etched on giant stones and displayed for everyone to see every day.

As a leader, I need to reinforce and make our organizational values visible, so they are reflected in the attitudes and actions of our team. This can be done in many ways, such as prominently displaying your values on your website, creating posters to hang in your office, or even having them printed on t-shirts or other items that your team members can wear.

- **Stories**

Stories are one of the most powerful tools for shaping culture. Jesus modeled this so well. Not only was he a compelling storyteller, but he was also a strategic storyteller. He used stories to reshape people's paradigms, including stories of extraordinary generosity (The Parable of the Good Samaritan, Luke 10:25–37), unrelenting prayer (The Parable of the Persistent Widow, Luke 18:1–8), and unprecedented forgiveness (The Parable of the Lost Son, Luke 15:11–32).

Procter & Gamble (P&G) is a multinational consumer goods company known for its diverse portfolio of products. Recognizing the power of storytelling as an effective means of communication, it has embraced it as part of its corporate culture, bringing in Hollywood directors to teach their executives the art of storytelling.

By hiring Hollywood directors, P&G aimed to impart the skills and techniques used in the entertainment industry to its executives. These directors possessed expertise in crafting compelling narratives that engage and captivate audiences. P&G recognized that executives who can effectively tell a good story can inspire and motivate their teams, influence stakeholders, and communicate the company's mission and values in a more memorable way.[2]

Stories are influential because they stick, spread, and shape your culture. To capitalize on the power of stories, consider the following:

Be a storyteller. I used to teach my trainers at the North American Mission Board to tell stories. But I didn't call them stories. I referred to them as "strategic narratives." I would challenge the trainers to tell a story at a strategic time, for a strategic reason, in a strategic way. Let all three of those phrases sink in because all three are essential. Crafting a strategic narrative involves more than just telling a story; it's about captivating your listeners right from the beginning. It's the art of creating tension, keeping listeners curious about the unfolding events of your story. Strategic narrative strikes the balance with just the right number of details, vividly portraying characters' personalities, physical attributes, and environment. The aim is to not only make listeners hear the story but to also visualize it. Finally, the narrative culminates in a powerful landing, forging a connection between the story's lesson and its application to the listener's own life or circumstances. Stories are entertaining, but that is not why we use them as leaders. We use stories in critical moments to help people learn and discover new insights.

Stories have power. They stick with you. They shape your thinking. And they can help you build a culture that reflects your values. What stories can you collect and share that will help your people understand the values of your organization? Sharing these stories will make your values clearer for your team.

Be a story historian. Some stories need to become legendary in your organization; stories that people will continue to tell years from now. These accounts reinforce common behaviors you want to see in your organization.

For example, everyone has heard legendary customer service stories from Ritz-Carlton, such as the story of the little boy who left Joshie, his stuffed giraffe, behind at the hotel. An employee found the beloved animal but, before shipping it back, clicked a few pictures of Joshie having an "extended vacation." When the giraffe was shipped back to the family, the box included photos of Joshie lounging by the pool, riding on the hotel golf cart, or getting a massage. Imagine the impression that simple act left on that family.[3]

The employees of Ritz-Carlton pride themselves on living up to these types of legendary stories. And that's what you want for your organization. You want stories that inspire and motivate your team to live out your values every day.

- **Be an Example**

Most importantly, values flow out of who you are as a leader. Your actions speak louder than your words. If you want your team to embody certain values, you must consistently model them. This means being intentional about your own behavior and holding yourself accountable to the same standards.

If you are not modeling the values, they will never become a part of your culture. Helping your team understand your culture is much more about living it than teaching it.

Communicating your values effectively is essential to creating a strong and cohesive team. So make your values visible, use stories to reinforce your values, and model the behavior you want to see. By doing so, you'll create a shared sense of purpose and direction that will drive your team toward creating a healthy culture.

> What can you do to increase the visibility of your organization's values?

> How are you currently using stories to shape the culture you desire? What can you do to improve the way you use stories to shape the culture of your organization?

> What is one value you feel is important for you to model for your team right now? Why?

Key #3: Expectation—Evaluate the Values

Evaluating the values is the third key to effectively shaping culture. It is not enough to simply create and leave a set of values hanging on a wall somewhere. Leaders must regularly evaluate how well they and their team are living out these values. Doing so helps identify where value drift is occurring and bring the values back into alignment.

There are various ways to evaluate values effectively. For instance, one of my pastor friends ensures that the church he leads conducts quarterly reviews with its staff. One part of the review process involves having the staff evaluate how well they currently exhibit the church's values.

At the end of every ninety-day interval, each staff member engages in a conversation with their respective supervisor. This dialogue encompasses a review of their progress toward established goals, as well as a reflective analysis of their alignment with the staff values: honor, grit, teachability, and critical thinking.

To facilitate this process, a structured worksheet is provided to the staff members, which serves as a foundational tool. This worksheet features distinct sections for each value. For example, within the

"Honor" section, the worksheet lists the components that constitute honor, such as:

- Respects the work of both supervisors and subordinates equally
- Treats others as he or she would like to be treated
- Does not misplace or misuse respect they receive
- Respects the time, talent, and treasure given by the dream team and members at large

Next, the staff members are prompted to provide specific instances of how they have demonstrated the value of honor. This exercise encourages self-reflection and empowers them to recognize their efforts in upholding this value.

Furthermore, the worksheet allocates space for the staff to articulate actionable steps for enhancing their embodiment of the value. This forward-looking component stimulates introspection and the formulation of growth strategies. Through this process, staff members can identify areas where the Holy Spirit is prompting them to strengthen their alignment with the core values.

Engaging in this comprehensive exercise at the conclusion of each ninety-day period serves as a powerful reinforcement mechanism. It reiterates the significance of the core values within the minds of the staff and bolsters their commitment to cultivating these values in their daily interactions and decisions.

Another effective way to evaluate values is to gather the team together, write the values on a whiteboard, and have everyone assign a grade as to how well they believe the team is doing with each value. Once everyone records their grades, the team can share their evaluations and combine their grades for each value. They can then discuss what is going well and what needs improvement and develop an action plan to integrate changes. This exercise is an excellent way to evaluate values and is included in this module's "Put It Into Practice" section.

Evaluating values regularly ensures that they remain relevant and impactful. It also helps to keep the team focused on what matters most and encourages everyone to stay accountable to the shared values.

How often do you and your team evaluate your organization's or group's values?

What specific strategies do you use to ensure that the values are being lived out consistently?

How can you ensure everyone is held accountable for adhering to the values and minimizing value drift?

Key #4: Conviction—Making Decisions Based on Values

Leaders who shape culture make decisions based on their values. When you make decisions that reflect your true convictions, you will inspire your team to follow suit.

Chick-fil-A is a great example of a company that made decisions based on its values and has been incredibly successful. In the late 1990s, Chick-fil-A executives analyzed the business environment and debated how to maintain a strong market share. They viewed Boston Market as their main competitor and were concerned about the competitor's aggressive expansion plan to top a billion in sales by 2000. The executives debated different strategies for getting bigger, but the founder and CEO, Truett Cathy, sat quietly at the end of the boardroom table, listening to the discussion.

Suddenly, Cathy banged his fist on the table, and everyone turned to him. He said, "You have been consumed with how to make Chick-fil-A bigger, how to grow. You are focusing on the wrong goal. You need to focus on how we can make our company *better*. If we are better, then our customers will demand for us to be bigger, and growth will come naturally."[4]

If you look at Chick-fil-A's values, you will notice that there is not one value about getting bigger, but all of them reflect on improving for the sake of their employees and customers:

> **We're here to serve.** We keep the needs of Operators, their Team Members and customers at the heart of our work, doing what is best for the business and best for them.
>
> **We're better together.** It's through teamwork and collaboration that we do our best work. We're an inclusive culture that leverages the strengths of our diverse talent to innovate and maximize our care for Operators, their Team Members and customers.
>
> **We are purpose-driven.** We model our Purpose every day, connecting our work and daily activities to our business strategy, supporting each other's efforts to be good stewards who create a positive impact on all who come in contact with Chick-fil-A.
>
> **We pursue what's next.** We find energy in adapting and re-inventing how we do things, from the way we work to how we care for others.[5]

Truett Cathy's words that day reflected the organization's core values and framed the company's direction from then on. Chick-fil-A became focused on how to improve its culture, customer service, and the various areas of its business. The obsession with growth faded, and a new focus on quality emerged. And as a result, in 2000, Boston Market filed for bankruptcy, and Chick-fil-A topped a billion dollars in sales!

Leaders who make decisions based on their values will create a culture that is aligned with their beliefs. When the team sees the leader making decisions based on the organization's values, they will feel more connected to the company's mission and will be more likely to follow suit. In the end, this will lead to a culture that is strong, authentic, and successful.

Key #5: Connection—Treat Your People Right

To shape a truly healthy culture, it is essential to focus on treating your people right. Your team members are not just responsible for delivering the culture you desire; they should also be beneficiaries of it. Values shouldn't just be exhibited for those you serve; they should also encompass how your team treats each other.

Let's consider an example of what it looks like for an organization to treat people right. Imagine a nonprofit called Community Care Foundation (CCF). They have four core values—empathy, collaboration, integrity, and impact that direct their actions.

Let's take a closer look at each.

- **Empathy**

CCF prioritizes understanding and connecting with individuals on a personal level, ensuring our programs address unique needs and challenges.

- **Collaboration**

Collaboration is fundamental, as CCF actively seeks partnerships and synergies with other organizations to amplify our impact and leverage resources.

- **Integrity**

CCF maintains the highest ethical standards, upholding transparency, honesty, and accountability in all our operations and interactions.

- **Impact**

CCF is dedicated to making a tangible and lasting impact by prioritizing evidence-based practices, measuring outcomes, and continuously evaluating our programs for effectiveness and meaningful change.

These values help guide CCF's decision-making as they pursue the vision of impacting the community. But they also want these values to be lived out internally as a team.

Here's how these same four values foster a positive work environment and enrich the lives of their employees.

- **Empathy**

By valuing empathy, CCF fosters a work environment where employees feel genuinely connected to each other as well as the individuals they serve.

- **Collaboration**

By fostering a collaborative culture, employees are encouraged to work together, leveraging their collective strengths and expertise. Through collaboration, employees feel valued and supported, leading to increased job satisfaction and professional growth.

- **Integrity**

By upholding transparency, honesty, and accountability, CCF builds a foundation of trust and respect among employees. This value ensures that employees can rely on one another, fostering a safe and supportive work environment. When individuals feel valued, respected, and trusted, they are empowered to bring their best selves to work, resulting in enhanced productivity, creativity, and overall job satisfaction.

- **Impact**

By valuing the impact we are making, CCF focuses on measurable outcomes and continuous improvement. By prioritizing evidence-based practices and regularly evaluating our programs and services, employees witness the tangible impact of their work. Seeing their contributions directly translate into positive change within the community creates a sense of fulfillment and pride.

Conclusion

When leaders learn to live their values both externally with those they serve and internally with their team, they create an environment where team members feel valued, heard, and supported.

Living your values with your team helps you to foster a culture of trust and collaboration, enabling everyone to thrive and contribute to the organization's success. Staying true to your values is vital in creating a culture that everyone takes pride in.

When team members feel valued and supported, they become motivated to deliver exceptional results and help the organization achieve its goals. A healthy culture not only benefits the mission but also enriches the lives of everyone involved.

Put It Into Practice

Developing a new skill requires practice. Before you get together with your trainer, complete some of the following assignments to help you practice shaping culture.

1. If you are considering starting a church, nonprofit, or business, take some time to write down four to six core values you want to see as part of the organization's culture. These values should be reflective of the kind of culture you want to establish and the goals you hope to achieve. Once you have identified these values, share them with a mentor, friend, or colleague, and get their feedback. Think about how you can make these values central to everything you do, from hiring and training employees to making key decisions.

2. Write down four to six core values you want to see as part of your family's culture. These values should be reflective of the kind of family you want to have and the goals you hope to achieve as a family. Once you have identified these values, discuss them with your family and get their input. Consider

how you can make these values a part of your daily life and use them to shape the way you interact with one another. Set aside regular family meetings to discuss how you are doing as a family in living out these values and to make any necessary adjustments.

3. Think of a person or organization whose culture you admire. Write down the values you believe are driving that culture. Then, think about ways that you can incorporate those values into your own life or organization. Consider how you can adapt those values to your unique situation and how you can make them central to everything you do.

4. Gather your team and evaluate how well you are living out the values of your organization's culture. Start by writing down your organization's values and giving it a letter grade of A, B, C, D, or E based on how well you believe you are living out that value. Do this individually and then come together to discuss your evaluations.

During the team discussion, identify any discrepancies or disagreements and work to reach a consensus on the grade for each value. Once you have agreed on the grades, work together to plan action steps to strengthen how you live out the values. Assign responsibilities for each action step and set deadlines for implementation.

Remember, the goal of this assignment is not to assign blame or criticize each other but rather to work together to identify areas where you can improve as a team and develop a plan to strengthen your culture.

Reflect on Your Learning

Where did you grow the most in this competency?

What next step do you need to take to continue to grow in this competency?

Meet With Your Trainer

Consistent practice can be a great beginning to sharpening a skill, but developing a skill also requires processing what you learned with others.

Meet with your trainer and discuss what you learned from this module.

Dig Deeper

If you are leading or participating in an internship or want to continue to grow in the competency of shaping culture, go to https://www.multiplygroup.org/internship-planner to download the companion guide to this book.

---

[1] Christina Folz, "How To Change Your Organizational Culture," *SHRM*, September 22, 2016, https://www.shrm.org/hr-today/news/hr-magazine/1016/pages/how-to-change-your-organizational-culture.aspx.

[2] Dan Schawbel, "How to Use Storytelling as a Leadership Tool," *Forbes*, August 13, 2012, https://www.forbes.com/sites/danschawbel/2012/08/13/how-to-use-storytelling-as-a-leadership-tool/#.

[3] Chris Hurn, "Stuffed Giraffe Shows What Customer Service Is All About," *HuffPost*, December 6, 2017, https://www.huffpost.com/entry/stuffed-giraffe-shows-wha_b_1524038.

[4] Phil Love, "Bigger is Not Always Better," *Pactola*, July 3, 2017, https://pactola.com/blog/2017/7/3/bigger-is-not-always-better.

[5] Chick-fil-A, "Our Values," https://www.chick-fil-a.com/careers/culture.

3

Casting Vision

As I (Mac) sat across from the church planter, I couldn't help but notice his striking appearance—at twenty-eight years old, he stood tall at six-foot-four, with chiseled features that spoke of determination and ambition. But I couldn't help but feel a sinking sensation in my stomach as he confidently declared his plans to have five hundred people at his opening service, which was only about eight weeks away.

I've been in this game for a while now, and I know that success doesn't come from just having a grand vision. As I listened to this young man's plans, I couldn't help but notice the gaps in his preparations. He had no leadership team in place, no assimilation process to engage the new crowd he was expecting, and just a small core group.

Don't get me wrong—I love being around young entrepreneurs who are full of energy and enthusiasm. But I've also seen my fair share of naive visionaries with great dreams but no practical plan to bring them to reality. And that's where the trouble starts.

Naive visionaries are dreamers who hope for great things but often fail to do the hard work that will turn their vision into reality. They overlook crucial details, fail to count the cost, and make assumptions that often lead to disappointment. Their unrealistic timelines and shortcuts can cause them to burn out quickly, leaving their vision unfulfilled.

One of the biggest problems with naive visionaries is that they often haven't taken the time to build a strong foundation of leadership and support. They assume that others are as invested in their vision as they are and become frustrated when they encounter resistance or delay. They may even presume God will fill in the gaps where they haven't done the necessary work.

In the end, naive visionaries rarely succeed in bringing their vision to life. Their lack of preparation and foresight leads to frustration, burnout, and failure. This is true whether they lead a church, a nonprofit, or a business.

I chuckle to myself as I think about the stark contrast between this young church planter and my friend Chris. Chris left the comfort of a staff position at a megachurch in the East to embark on a risky journey of church planting in Denver.

He wasn't just a dreamer; he put in the work to prepare for the dream. He counted the cost, and he counted it well. He underwent an intense assessment and enrolled in a church planter cohort training process to prepare himself for the challenges ahead. He didn't leave anything to chance. He secured a team of prayer warriors and a church-planting coach, as well as meticulously studying the context of Denver before even setting foot there.

But that wasn't all. Chris knew the biggest challenge he would face would be financing, so he put together a thorough plan and went into fundraising efforts. His effort resulted in over a year's worth of his projected budget in the bank. He didn't stop there; he upped his networking game and met with anybody and everybody he could. Even in the midst of the 2020 pandemic, Chris's determination didn't waver. He used social media and a small network of people in Denver to expand his relationships.

By the time Chris moved to Denver, he had built a strong foundation. He knew the city like the back of his hand and had a solid leadership team in place. And even in the face of adversity, Chris's church continued to grow and reach people in his community. Chris's story stands in stark contrast to the naive visionaries who only dream without doing the necessary groundwork.

In Scripture, we witness God bestowing visions upon his chosen leaders. To Abraham, he revealed a vision of a great nation; Moses, a glimpse of the Promised Land; Nehemiah, a profound vision of a restored Jerusalem; and Paul, a calling to spread the message of the gospel. Similarly, God gives leaders a vision for local church ministry, nonprofits, and businesses. As those in leadership positions, it's our responsibility to invest the time to discern God's heart and capture his vision.

It's important to note that we're talking about *God's* vision here and not necessarily the vision of the leader. Sometimes leaders can run hard after a personal vision that may be steeped in pride, selfish ambition, insecurity, or a fear of people. Or they may be tempted to run after all sorts of good things but miss out on God's vision for their work. Others may have clarity on the vision at first but, due to a myriad of factors, get off track and start pursuing something else entirely. As leaders, our competency lies in being able to communicate a clear picture of the future in a way that motivates others to take steps that advance the God-given vision. In this module, we will explore the practices necessary for leaders to successfully move their organization toward God's vision.

First, let's work to define the character and competency that help cast vision:

Character: *Submission*
Leaders listen to God's voice, know God's heart, and obediently follow God's will.

Competency: *Casting Vision*
Communicate a clear picture of the future in a way that motivates others to take actions that advance the God-given vision.

Objectives

1. Develop a greater understanding of the importance of submission in leadership and how it relates to casting vision.
2. Learn how to create a clear and compelling vision for your organization using the Vision Scope framework.
3. Understand the importance of long-, mid-, and short-range vision, and learn how to create outcomes that align with each time horizon.
4. Be able to identify potential distractions and dangers that could derail your vision and develop strategies for avoiding or overcoming them.
5. Gain practical experience in casting vision by completing one or more of the suggested assignments in the "Put It Into Practice" section and receiving feedback from others.

Deepen Your Character: *Submission*

Leadership is a unique position; it allows us to hear and participate in God's vision. While the vision is from God, he works through our individual gifts, personalities, and strengths to bring it to fruition. However, we must be careful not to take ownership of the vision. This can feed our ego, make us self-reliant and proud, become the basis of our identity, and lead us to compare ourselves to others. Vision can become addictive, driving us to work harder than God intends and leading us to worship the vision rather than the Giver of the vision.

To combat these tendencies, leaders must grow in a spirit of submission. A leader listens to God's voice, knows God's heart, and obediently follows God's will. This character trait is exemplified in the Apostle Paul, who faced a critical moment of decision in his ministry. In Acts 16, Paul and his team planned to preach the gospel in the province of Asia, but the Holy Spirit prevented them from doing so. They then attempted to go to Bithynia, but again the Holy Spirit did not allow them. In the midst of these closed doors, Paul received a vision in which a man from Macedonia pleaded with him, "Come over to Macedonia and help us" (v. 9).

At this point, Paul could have easily insisted on his own agenda and plans, but instead, he submitted to God's plan. He and his team immediately set out for Macedonia. Paul's submission led to the spread of Christianity into Europe and the Western world and opened up a whole new mission field he could not have anticipated.

As we seek to grow in submitting to God, it's important to be aware of potential traps that can hinder our progress. Let's consider three "submission saboteurs" we need to watch out for.

The Comparison Trap

When we start comparing ourselves to others, we can become focused on our own achievements and lose sight of God's vision. Instead of trying to keep up with others, let's focus on being faithful to what God has called us to do.

The Distraction Trap

We live in a world full of distractions, and it's easy to lose sight of God's voice in the midst of all the noise. We can be so busy doing the work of God that we can miss out on the voice of God. So let's intentionally create space in our lives to listen and remain focused on God's direction and guidance.

The People-Pleasing Trap

It's natural to want to be liked and respected by others, but when we prioritize pleasing people over following God's will, we can compromise our values and lose sight of God's direction. The pressure to please or impress those we lead can lead to a spirit of pride. We may even find ourselves submitting to the will of the majority or the will of key influencers in our lives rather than submitting to God. This dangerous path can lead us away from God's plan and into disobedience. Let's prioritize pleasing God above all else and trust that he will take care of the rest.

As Christian leaders, we must be intentional in developing a spirit of submission to God. It requires us to let go of our own agenda, to humbly listen to God's voice, and to follow his will faithfully. We can cultivate a heart that is fully surrendered to him by avoiding the submission saboteurs of comparison, distraction, and people-pleasing.

Scripture

As you read the following Scripture, meditate on what the author wishes to communicate and answer the questions below. Allow the Holy Spirit to speak to you and challenge you as a leader about how you can develop your character so that you are continually submitting to God.

Acts 16:6-10

Paul and his companions traveled throughout the region of Phrygia and Galatia, having been kept by the Holy Spirit from preaching the word in the province of Asia. When they came to the border of Mysia, they tried to enter Bithynia, but the Spirit of Jesus would not allow them to. So they passed by Mysia and went down to Troas. During the night Paul had a vision of a man of Macedonia standing and begging him, "Come over to Macedonia and help us." After Paul had seen the vision, we got ready at once to leave for Macedonia, concluding that God had called us to preach the gospel to them.

> God prevented Paul's team from returning to Asia twice before revealing his plan for them to go to Macedonia. What emotions do you imagine Paul felt when he was prevented from moving forward with his plan? In what ways can you relate to Paul's situation?

What do you think would have been the most difficult part for Paul in submitting to this change of plans?

Which of the "submission saboteurs" do you struggle with the most (Comparison Trap, Distraction Trap, or People-Pleasing Trap), and how can you work to combat it?

How can you create space in your life to intentionally listen for God's direction and guidance?

In what specific areas of your leadership or vision do you need to intentionally create space to listen for God's direction and guidance?

Now that we have examined the character trait of submission, we can begin to work through the core competency for this module: *casting vision*. As you read what follows, note how submission can undergird a leader's competency of casting vision.

Develop Your Competency: *Casting Vision*
Preassessment

Before proceeding, complete the assessment below. In the final module of this training guide, you will retake it as a postassessment to measure your transformation and growth in this competency.

The following proficiencies demonstrate mastery of this module's competency. For each of them, give yourself a grade of A, B, C, D, or E to reflect your actual level of competency today. Giving yourself an A+ indicates you are a model for others to follow. An E indicates no mastery.

Proficiency	Preassessment
I prioritize prayer and dependence on God in capturing and communicating his vision for my organization or team.	
I articulate a clear and compelling vision that inspires others to take action.	
I identify and communicate opportunities and potential distractions in a way that aligns with the mission and values of my organization.	
I develop specific goals and objectives that help bring the vision to life.	
I regularly evaluate progress toward the vision and make necessary adjustments to keep the team on track.	

Which of the five proficiencies do you want to grow in the most? Why is it important for you to grow in that aspect?

How has your ability to cast a clear and compelling vision improved over time?

In what ways have you relied on your own strength and understanding rather than seeking God's guidance and direction in casting a vision for your organization?

Capturing God's Vision for Your Organization

Have you ever been on a road trip with a clear destination in mind, but every step of the journey was filled with excitement? Cindy and I (Mac) felt exactly that when we decided to take a drive along the stunning Pacific Coast Highway (PCH) from San Diego to San Francisco. Our primary vision was reaching San Francisco, but we were equally excited about the incredible experiences we'd have along the way.

Driving up the PCH, we encountered unforgettable milestones that made the whole trip as thrilling as reaching our destination. One of the highlights was our stop in Orange County, where we took a leisurely stroll along Balboa Island's boardwalk, admiring the unique homes along the waterway. Trust me; you've got to experience it at least once!

In LA, we couldn't miss the chance to see the iconic Hollywood sign up close. Driving up there and capturing the moment with loads of photos was epic. Another milestone was hiking the Channel Islands off the coast of Santa Barbara. The breathtaking views and rugged landscapes left us in awe of God's beauty.

Capturing God's vision for your organization is just like going on that thrilling road trip. Along the way, you'll encounter amazing milestones as you work toward fulfilling God's plan.

To discover his vision, spend time in prayer, dive deep into the Word, and have strategy sessions with your key leaders. It's like watching a painter create a masterpiece—God will reveal the ultimate destination for your organization and unveil key milestones that will mark your progress.

When we started Multiply Group, we knew God's ultimate destination for us was equipping leaders in organizations to develop a culture of reproducing healthy leaders. We noticed that many leaders were being developed haphazardly, unintentionally, or by chance. So, our divine mission is to change this paradigm, making discipling of leaders the norm among staff and volunteer leaders. We wholeheartedly embrace this calling, aiming to create a lasting impact by instilling intentional processes throughout organizations.

But our journey is not just about the final destination; we're also super excited about the milestones along the way. For instance, we plan to certify thirty coaches in our training processes in the next three years, expanding our impact. We also want to enhance our discipleship resource library, offering organizations even more options to disciple their leaders. And that's not all! We've got several other God-inspired milestones we're eagerly pursuing.

Creating a vision statement is common practice for organizations. Ikea's vision statement is "to create a better everyday life for the many people,"[1] while Southwest Airlines' mission is "to be the world's most loved, most efficient, and most profitable airline."[2]

But vision isn't just a statement; it's a journey with a clear destination and multiple exciting milestones along the way. Vision should be a captivating story that motivates and engages everyone involved. Seeing it this way fosters a sense of shared ownership and purpose among team members, which is vital for any organization's success.

To help you and your organization create a clear and inspiring vision, my buddy David Putman and I (Mac) devised a framework called the Vision Scope. Picture it like a periscope on a ship, providing you with a comprehensive view of your (vision) journey.

Vision Scope

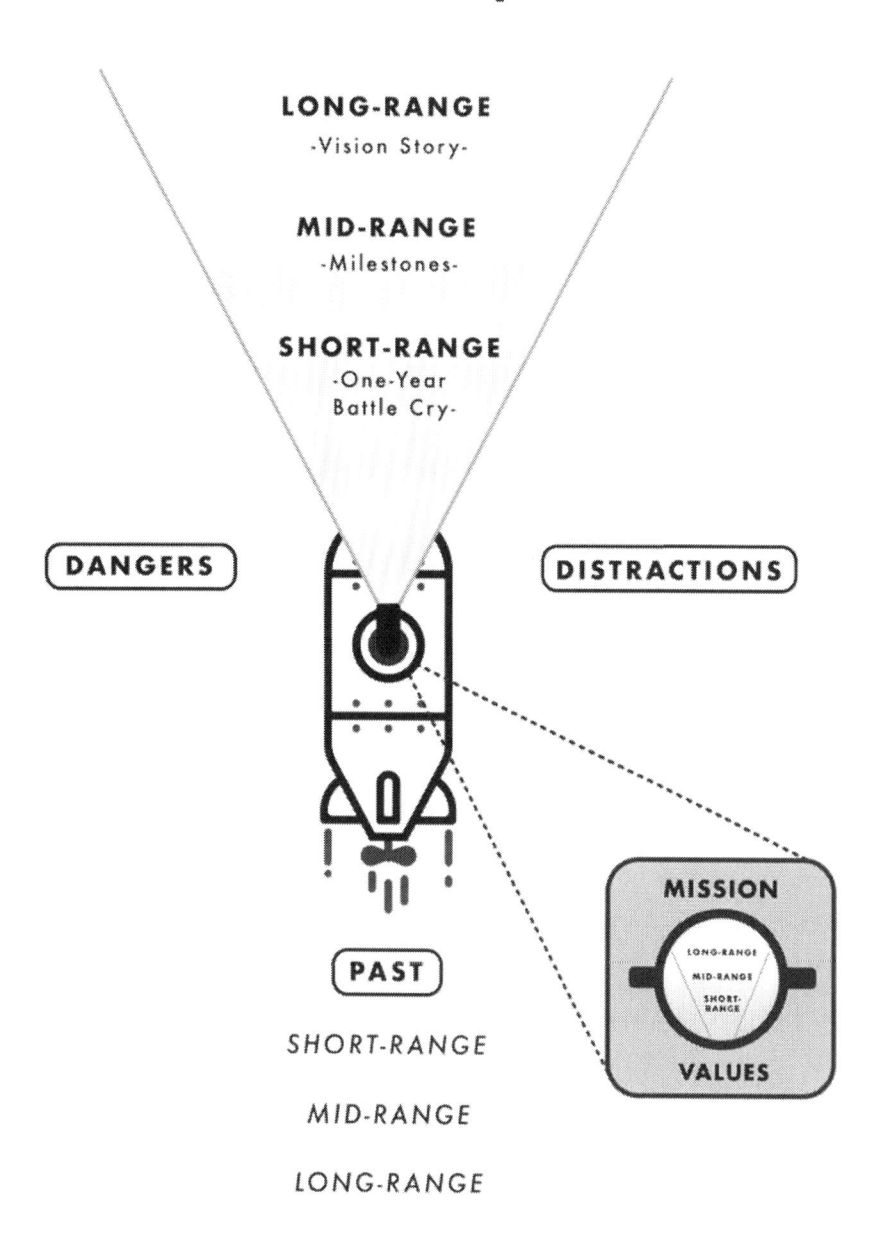

LONG-RANGE
-Vision Story-

MID-RANGE
-Milestones-

SHORT-RANGE
-One-Year
Battle Cry-

(DANGERS)   (DISTRACTIONS)

(PAST)

SHORT-RANGE

MID-RANGE

LONG-RANGE

MISSION
LONG-RANGE
MID-RANGE
SHORT-RANGE
VALUES

At the top of the Vision Scope is your mission statement, which concisely explains why your organization exists. Your mission statement helps everyone on your team know why you do what you do as an organization. Generally, it's something that never changes. So, envision your mission statement to be etched at the top of your Vision Scope, guiding your ship toward your ultimate destination.

The bottom of the Vision Scope is where your values are etched. As we discussed in the second module, values are the consistent behaviors that help you stay aligned with your mission as you journey toward your vision. On a ship, the periscope is a crucial navigation tool. It allows you to see and steer where you are headed and turns in various directions to give you a 360-degree view, keeping you safe on your journey.

Looking through the Vision Scope into the future is where the real magic happens. You get to see where your organization is headed in the long run—way out into the distance toward the ultimate destination. But it doesn't stop there. On the horizon, you can also see a mid-range view of significant milestones you will pass on your journey. These milestones become like guideposts, helping you track progress and ensure you're on the right path. And if you switch your gaze a little closer, you can even see things that are in the near future, within the next year or so. Looking through the Vision Scope, you can see where God is taking your organization in the long-, mid-, and short-ranges.

Turning the Vision Scope 180 degrees allows you to see where you've been. Reflecting on the past is crucial for learning, celebrating achievements, and understanding what worked and what didn't.

Turning it 90 degrees to the right reveals potential distractions that could veer you off course from your mission and vision. These distractions might be tempting, but they can lead you away from what truly matters. Turning 90 degrees to the left reveals dangers and threats to your mission, like financial downturns or internal conflicts among staff. These dangers can seriously harm your organizational vision if not addressed.

Crafting a compelling vision story is key to guiding and inspiring your team toward your God-given vision. This module will walk you through essential Vision Scope questions to help you craft your vision story. To make it practical, we've included a sample from "Hope For All," a fictional nonprofit organization, to illustrate the components of a powerful vision story. (This sample can be found on pages 103–107, at the end of this module.)

Pray First and Always

Before delving into the questions that shape your vision, it is essential to emphasize that the entire process hinges on prayer. Prayer is not merely a significant aspect of leadership; it serves as the lifeline that intimately connects us with the heart of God. As leaders, we are entrusted with a higher calling beyond the pursuit of organizational success; we are called to be vessels of God's kingdom, devoted to fulfilling his divine purposes. Thus, seeking his guidance through prayer is paramount. Nehemiah's story serves as a profound example of a leader who drew strength from prayer to capture God's heart and vision. Touched by the plight of Jerusalem's broken walls, Nehemiah's immediate response was prayer and fasting. He dedicated months to seeking God's guidance before presenting his vision to King Artaxerxes and the people of Israel (Nehemiah 1–2).

We can easily fall into the trap of relying solely on our own abilities and expertise. We can get so busy doing God's work that we forget to seek God's guidance and direction. However, this dangerous path can lead us away from God's purposes for our organization. We must be intentional about setting aside time to pray and listen to his voice. Even when we make mistakes or take wrong turns, we can trust that God will guide us back to his path. As we seek God's heart and vision through prayer, we will find that our leadership becomes more effective and aligned with his purposes.

Now that we've established prayer as the basis, let's consider six primary questions from the Vision Scope framework that will help you craft your vision story.

Question #1: What Is Our Mission?

Before you can clarify your vision, you must know your mission. The mission is a statement that explains why your organization exists. It's crucial because it keeps you on course as you drive toward your vision. Here are a few examples of mission statements:

> **Church:** 901 Church, Memphis. *We exist so that people would be reached and lives would be changed.*[3]

> **Nonprofit:** World Vision. *To follow our Lord and Savior Jesus Christ in working with the poor and oppressed to promote human transformation, seek justice, and bear witness to the good news of the Kingdom of God.*[4]

> **Business:** Hobby Lobby. *Offering customers exceptional selection and value. Serving our employees and their families by establishing a work environment and company policies that build character, strengthen individuals, and nurture families.*[5]

While the mission statement is brief, it doesn't mean it comes easily. In our experience, Rick and I have both had to wrestle in prayer to get a full grip on the mission statement for the organizations we've started. We often describe this process as birthing. We pray, grapple, think, and write different versions of the mission statement. We go through a lot of paper—throwing away various drafts, and then one day, it comes. And when it does, it captures our hearts.

Whether it comes easily or not, you must be a passionate owner of the mission. It's the guiding force that keeps you on target with the vision. Think of it this way: mission is your purpose (a statement), and vision is what happens as you live out your mission (a story). You will use the Vision Scope tool to help you craft a vision story.

We recommend focusing on four key elements to determine your organization's mission. These elements are critical in helping you answer the question: What is our mission? Writing a description of all four elements will be helpful in creating a mission statement that captures your organization's purpose and provides a clear direction for your team. If you do not have a mission statement for your organization, use our Mission Statement tool to write your mission statement. You can find this at www.multiplygroup.org/leadinganorganization.

- **Element #1: Passion**

Your passion should drive your mission, serving as a powerful motivator to persevere through challenges. Reflect on what deeply inspires both you and your team. Write a compelling description of the passion that drives your organization. Reflect on what motivates you and your team, the values that fuel your commitment, and the beliefs you hold dear.

- **Element #2: Strengths**

To fulfill your mission effectively, it's crucial to recognize and leverage your organization's competencies and resources. Identify the unique skills and expertise that your organization brings to the table. In the Mission Statement tool (www.multiplygroup.org/leadinganorganization), describe your organization's strengths and competencies. Highlight the unique skills and expertise that set you apart. Identify the resources and capabilities that enable you to fulfill your mission effectively.

- **Element #3: Problem**

Clearly identify the specific problem or need that your organization is ideally positioned to address. In the Mission Statement tool, write a clear and concise description of the specific problem or need that your organization is best suited to address. By narrowing your focus, you enable your organization to have a more profound impact, making a difference where it matters most.

- **Element #4: Holy Spirit promptings**

As mentioned earlier, your organization's mission should be birthed through prayer and guided by the Holy Spirit. Engage in prayerful contemplation as you discern God's calling for your organization. Listen to the promptings of the Holy Spirit and seek divine guidance. In the Mission Statement tool, write about the promptings and insights you sense from the Holy Spirit. Reflect and consider what God is leading you to accomplish. Write down any Scripture passages the Holy Spirit has impressed upon your heart in regard to your mission.

After processing these four elements, you can craft a one-sentence mission statement that reflects your organization's purpose and direction. This statement should be concise and memorable, but most importantly, it should capture the heart of your organization. Remember, your mission is your purpose, and your vision is what happens as you live out your mission.

How does your organization's mission statement inform your day-to-day decisions and actions? Are there any areas where you feel it falls short or needs improvement?

If you don't currently have a mission statement, try using our Mission Statement Tool. Share your draft with a mentor or colleague and get their feedback.

Question #2: What Are the Core Values of Our Organization?

As we delve into the Vision Scope, it's important to revisit the concept of core values, which we covered in detail in the second module of this book. Core values are the guiding principles that define the behaviors and attitudes that keep us aligned with God's vision. We often refer to these as "core behaviors" because they represent how we will behave. These behaviors paint a picture for our team of what is expected and what mentality to use when filtering decisions. As leadership specialist Simon Sinek aptly puts it, "Values are verbs, not nouns. In order to build the culture we envision, we have to enact our values in how we show up every single day."[6]

When defining your core values, it's important to take time and process what core behaviors are essential to accomplishing your mission. Consider the behaviors you expect from your team and the actions that help you stay aligned with God's vision for your organization. We recommend having a maximum of five core values that everyone on your team can agree upon and get behind.

Once you define the values, it's time to live and reinforce them, as your values become the grid for making important decisions. In essence, your core values are the behaviors that, when lived out, keep you in alignment with the vision God has given you. For more information on how to use your values to guide decision-making, see my (Mac) book *Leading a Department*, module three.[7]

Now that you've established your mission statement and core values, it's time to start building the vision for your organization. But before we do that, let's turn the Vision Scope around and look at the past. This is important because where you've been can give you rich insight into where God is taking you as an organization.

Question #3: Where Have We Been (Rearview)?

Now, let's practice using the Vision Scope to get a good look at your organization's history and see what you can learn that will help you with your organization's future vision. As you look through the lens of the Vision Scope toward your past, you will ask: Where have we been? Looking back is essential, especially for existing organizations. If you're starting a new organization, reflecting on your past and what God has done in your life is also crucial. For now, let's focus on existing organizations.

When looking at your history, you can view it from three different ranges.

First, we set our sights on the *long-range* history. Picture a grand saga spanning five years and beyond. It's a tale of remarkable accomplishments etched in the annals of your organization. These achievements stand as testaments to your mission, values, and God's hand at work among you. They're the stories that will be passed down through generations, whispering wisdom and inspiration to fuel your future vision.

Now, let's shift our gaze a little closer. The *mid-range* view of your history encompasses the past two to four years. Here, you delve into the triumphs and troubles that have colored your journey. Each victory and challenge has left its mark, shaping and transforming your organization. Consider how these experiences have influenced your direction and trajectory. Here you'll uncover the lessons they hold and become a better, stronger team that God uses to win even greater victories in the future.

Now there's more to discover! As you continue to look at the history through the Vision Scope, refocus to look at the *short-range* history—the past year, a chapter teeming with fresh insights and exciting advancements. Consider what God has done through your organization in the past twelve months. Reflect on the challenges you faced and the victories you celebrated. These recent experiences provide valuable insight into the new things God is doing in and through your organization. They serve as beacons of hope, guiding your steps into a future brimming with potential.

It's vital to not cast aside the past and solely fixate on the future. As you peer through the scope behind you, you have a unique opportunity to celebrate and recalibrate. Celebrating wins keeps your spirits high, igniting the fires of motivation and keeping you steadfast on your mission. And recalibrating ensures you stay on track with God's grand vision for your organization, adjusting your sails to catch the winds of his guidance.

> Now, take some time to fill out the Rearview: Where have we been? section of the Vision Scope tool.

Question #4: Where Are We Headed (Forward View)?

Let's dive into the next part of the Vision Scope process and shift our gaze toward the future. Imagine it like peering through a periscope, exploring what lies ahead. We're going to venture into three dimensions: the long-range view, the mid-range milestones, and the short-range battle cry. As we progress through this process, it is vital to maintain alignment with our mission and values. These essential pillars will act as our guiding compass, ensuring that our vision remains true to our purpose and principles.

- **The long-range view**

On your Vision Scope tool, you will record your long-range vision in two ways: First, write a *compelling statement* summarizing the vision. This can help make the vision memorable and succinct. Second, you will write a *descriptive paragraph*. This is a paragraph that describes your vision in a more robust story format.

In the long-range view, you will envision where your organization is heading in five years or more. While the details may be challenging to see from this distance, you can identify your final destination. As you think through this dimension of your vision, pray hard and dream big.

Let's start with the *compelling statement*. The compelling statement should be concise yet captivating—just a few words that pack a punch and leave a lasting impression. It's your chance to express your organization's core vision in a way that inspires everyone who hears it.

Use bold and broad language to describe the difference you feel God is calling your organization to make. The focus should be on the overall impact you want to have. For instance, here are three examples of a compelling statement summarizing a long-range vision:

A Christian bookstore: *Enrich spiritual formation within our community by offering an abundant selection of the finest Christian resources available.*

A nonprofit: *Nurture a hunger-free community, where nourishment, friendship, and hope abound.*

An organization (Multiply Group): *Revolutionize the development of leaders by making discipling of leaders a normative behavior for staff and volunteer leaders.*

Bold statements like these inspire your team and help them understand the significant calling of being part of your organization.

Your long-range vision is like your organization's North Star. It should be ambitious and inspirational, guiding your team toward a future that aligns with God's calling.

Alongside the compelling statement, you'll craft a *descriptive paragraph*, which paints a vibrant picture of the future you envision. It describes your vision in a more robust and thorough way. Use descriptive language and specific details to make it engaging and relatable. You want to bring your vision story to life in a way that excites and motivates those who hear it. This can be one paragraph or you may choose to write a few paragraphs to clearly paint a picture of the future vision.

For example, for Multiply Group, our descriptive paragraphs say:

We envision a revolution in leadership development. We see a day when discipling of leaders is a normative behavior for staff and volunteer leaders. A future where Christian leaders at all levels of the leadership pipeline possess the confidence, competence, and tools necessary to disciple other leaders, propelling them to greater heights of leadership. By sowing the seeds of our transformative systems, we witness churches, nonprofits, and Christian-run businesses flourishing with healthy leadership, robust development programs, and the fruitful emergence of new leaders.

As this revolutionary movement gathers momentum, we are seeing organizations that are models of leadership development rapidly emerging in major cities worldwide as they wholeheartedly embrace our systems. This movement fuels the advancement of the Gospel and catalyzes church planting as we empower organizations to multiply leaders and expand their influence.

Moreover, we foster a strong community of Multiply Group coaches and organizations, fostering a collaborative learning and growth culture. With our renowned Multiply Group content as the go-to resource for leadership development in the US, Canada, Australia, and the UK, we stand at the forefront, shaping the future of Christian leadership and paving the way for a world transformed by empowered leaders.

As you work on your long-range vision, let your imaginations run wild! Think about what God wants your organization to achieve and become in the next five years and beyond.

Your compelling statement and descriptive paragraph (story) should capture the essence of your long-range vision. These will drive your aspirations and provide a clear direction for your organization's future.

Take your time to engage in thoughtful discussion and unleash your creativity. And be bold! Dare to dream big and aim high. With faith and God's guidance, there's no limit to what you can achieve. This exercise is your opportunity to chart a course for a future that aligns perfectly with your mission and values.

- **Mid-range milestones**

Alright, let's dive even deeper into the Vision Scope! It's time to shift our focus to the mid-range view of your organization's vision.

Just picture it: you're peering through the Vision Scope, and what do you see? It's a landscape filled with exciting mid-range milestones. These milestones are like mini destinations along your journey. They are some of the most important things your organization will accomplish in the next two to four years.

Reaching each milestone becomes a cause for celebration and a stepping stone toward the long-range vision. What was once a distant goal now becomes a tangible accomplishment, fueling your motivation and driving your organization forward.

We recommend choosing anywhere from three to five significant mid-range milestones. These milestones become guideposts, reminding you of your progress and keeping you on track toward your long-range vision.

So, let your imagination soar as you envision these mid-range milestones for your organization. Set your sights on the remarkable destinations you want to reach in the next two to four years. Each milestone achieved brings you closer to your long-range vision and propels your organization toward even greater success. For examples of mid-range milestones see the Hope For All Vision Scope at the end of this module.

Below are some tips to infuse a little more energy and engagement in your mid-range milestones:

Rally your team. Remember, this process is a team effort! Get everyone involved and excited about creating these faith-driven milestones. When you collaborate and unite toward common objectives, you enhance your chances of accomplishing your goals and witnessing extraordinary results.

Align with your mission. Choose major initiatives that resonate with your mission and align harmoniously with your long-range vision. These milestones should pack a powerful punch, contributing significantly to the overall impact you desire to make in the world.

Craft captivating descriptions. Condense each milestone into one or two captivating sentences. These concise statements will serve as beacons of inspiration for your team and potential donors, keeping everyone focused and motivated as you journey toward these transformative objectives.

Be specific and measurable. Avoid vague aspirations such as "increase outreach efforts." Instead, be specific and incorporate measurable numbers. For example, challenge yourselves with a goal such as "increase baptisms by 25 percent in the next three years." Clear metrics empower you to track progress effectively and stay on target.

Embrace adaptability. Although setting specific milestones is essential, remember that flexibility is key. Circumstances change, and unexpected challenges may arise along the way. Stay nimble and open to adjusting your milestones when necessary. This adaptive mindset will ensure you stay on course, even in the face of uncertainty.

With clarity, commitment, and the collective efforts of your team, you'll make remarkable progress toward the God-given vision that guides your organization.

- **Short-range battle cry**

It's time to get up close and personal with your vision! You've already set your sights on the long-range vision and crafted your compelling statement and descriptive paragraph. Next, you identified the exciting mid-range milestones for the next two to four years. Let's bring it closer and focus on the one-year view.

Within this one-year scope, God has planted a burning priority in your hearts—a specific focus that you want your team to conquer within the next twelve months. We call it the one-year battle cry. This battle cry will guide you, keeping you focused, motivated, and accountable. It's important because it gives you crystal-clear direction, ignites a sense of urgency, connects the dots between your short-range and long-range visions, brings accountability, and enables you to take tangible steps toward your mid-range and long-range vision.

There are three simple steps for creating your one-year battle cry. See a sample of the one-year battle cry from the nonprofit Hope For All at the end of this module.

Step 1. Craft a compelling and concise statement that summarizes your battle cry. This statement should capture the essence of your single focus for the year and make it memorable for everyone involved.

Step 2. Identify four to six measurable key objectives that support your battle cry. These objectives should be specific and quantifiable. They will serve as indicators of your progress throughout the year.

Step 3. Assign each key objective to a person or a department in your organization to take ownership of that key objective. By assigning responsibilities, you ensure that everyone knows their role in achieving the one-year objectives and foster a sense of accountability and collaboration.

Step 4. Use team meetings to regularly discuss the progress toward the one-year battle cry objectives. This will help keep everyone focused and motivated. One year may feel like a long time, but it is easy to get off course, so make sure you check the progress of the objectives at least every ninety days, if not even more frequently.

By following these steps, you can create a one-year battle cry that will help you achieve your big-picture priority for the year and keep your team focused, motivated, and accountable as they work toward the annual objectives.

Question #5: What Opportunities Are Presenting Themselves That May Be Distractions and Could Get Us Off Course (Starboard View)?

Now, let's explore the third view offered by the Vision Scope tool—think of it as turning the scope to the right or starboard side of the ship. As we look to the right, we encounter distractions—those alluring opportunities that have the potential to lead us off course or misalign with our core values.

For a church, a distraction might manifest as an attractive but time-consuming event that doesn't contribute to the congregation's spiritual growth. Although it may seem enticing to invest resources and energy into such endeavors, they could divert us from our primary purpose of nurturing faith and building a strong community.

In a business context, distractions can present themselves in various forms. It might involve chasing after every new market trend or investing in projects that don't align with our core competencies. These distractions might promise short-term gains or appear to be exciting ventures, but they have the potential to steer us away from our primary objectives and dilute our focus.

We must remain vigilant to safeguard our mission and values as we analyze and discern these distractions. Identifying and addressing these temptations will allow us to stay steadfast on our chosen path and ensure that our efforts are channeled effectively toward our true vision.

Use the Vision Scope tool to answer question #5 to identify opportunities that may be a distraction from your organization's vision.

Question #6: What Are the Dangers We Need to Be Aware of as We Move Forward (Port View)?

Now, let's turn our attention to the left, or port side, where we'll find the dangers—the threats that pose risks to our vision. For a church, internal dangers could include conflicts within the congregation, lack of effective leadership, or complacency in pursuing outreach and community service. External dangers may include declining attendance trends, changing societal values, or financial instability.

In business, dangers can also arise from within and outside the organization. Internally, challenges might include poor financial management, inefficient processes, or a disengaged workforce. Externally, dangers could manifest as intense competition, disruptive technological advancements, or economic recessions.

Remember, distractions can lead us astray, and dangers can derail our efforts. Acknowledging and addressing them strengthens our ability to stay focused, resilient, and aligned with our mission and values.

> Use the Vision Scope tool to answer question #6 to identify potential dangers to your organization's vision.

The Vision Scope is a powerful navigation tool that guides you on your journey toward God's preferred future for your organization. With the mission and values etched deeply into the Vision Scope, it serves as an instrument to keep your organization going in the right direction. Looking through the lens of the Vision Scope, organizations gain the wisdom of their past, discern any potential distractions, and recognize the dangers that can sneak up without warning.

As you pray and peer forward, the Vision Scope reveals a God-sized long-range vision, mid-range milestones, and short-range battle cry. Crafting your vision through this remarkable tool imparts clarity and precision, enabling you to articulate your organizational vision with unwavering confidence. With the Vision Scope as your navigation tool, you're not just casting visions; you're illuminating the path of the exciting journey God has for your organization.

Put It Into Practice
Developing a new skill requires practice. Before you get together with your trainer, complete a few of the following assignments to help you practice casting vision.

1. Schedule a prayer retreat to seek God's vision for your organization or future venture. Spend time in solitude, seeking God's guidance through prayer, and then meet with your trainer to share what God revealed to you.

2. Write a mission statement for your organization or revise your current one by focusing on four key elements—passion, strengths, problem, and Holy Spirit promptings. This statement should capture the heart of your organization and provide a clear direction for your team. After creating or revising your mission statement, share it with your trainer for feedback and guidance.

3. Develop an "elevator pitch" for your vision: craft a thirty-second pitch that communicates your vision clearly and concisely. This is a great exercise to practice communicating your vision to others and ensuring it is easily understandable and compelling. Share that elevator pitch with your trainer to get their feedback.

4. Working with your team, choose a one-year battle cry for your organization, which will serve as the main focus for the next twelve months. Write a summary statement that clearly and concisely states the big priority focus for the year. Next, identify four to five key objectives that will support the one-year battle cry and help achieve it. These objectives should be specific and measurable, with clear timelines and assigned responsibilities. Ensure everyone on your team understands how their department and role tie into achieving the one-year battle cry. Once you have identified the one-year battle cry and key objectives, share these with your trainer.

5. Hold a vision-casting meeting: schedule a meeting with your team to cast the vision and gain buy-in. Use the Vision Scope, the one-year battle cry, and the side-view questions to guide the meeting. This will help everyone understand the vision, how it relates to their roles, and how they can contribute to its achievement.

Reflect on Your Learning

Where did you grow the most in this competency?

What next step do you need to take to continue to grow in this competency?

Meet With Your Trainer

Consistent practice can be a great beginning to sharpening a skill, but developing a skill also requires processing what you learned with others.

Meet with your trainer and discuss what you learned from this module.

Dig Deeper

If you are leading or participating in an internship or want to continue to grow in the competency of casting vision, go to https://www.multiplygroup.org/internship-planner to download the companion guide to this book.

---

[1] "The Ikea vision and values," *Ikea*, https://www.ikea.com/gb/en/this-is-ikea/about-us/the-ikea-vision-and-values-pub9aa779d0.

[2] "About Southwest Airlines," *Southwest*, https://www.southwest.com/about-southwest/.

[3] "Why We Exist," *901 Church*, https://901church.com/why-we-exist.

[4] "Mission & Values," *World Vision*, https://www.worldvision.org/about-us/mission-statement.

[5] "Hobby Lobby Mission Statement," *Zippia*, https://www.zippia.com/hobby-lobby-careers-26333/mission-statement/#.

[6] Simon Sinek (@simonsinek), "Values are verbs, not nouns. In order to build the culture we envision, we have to enact our values in how we show up every single day," Twitter post, May 21, 2021, https://twitter.com/simonsinek/status/1398040588025466881.

[7] Mac Lake, *Leading a Department: Developing the Character and Competency to Lead a Ministry* (Cody, WY: 100 Movements Publishing, 2022).

Hope For All (Sample Mission Statement)

Here's a sample of how Hope For All responded to the four elements of passion, strengths, problem, and Holy Spirit prompting to arrive at their mission statement:

- **Passion**

Hope For All is deeply driven by a passion for alleviating suffering and providing hope to those facing adversity. We believe that every individual deserves a chance to build a better future and that no one should be deprived of essential resources and opportunities.

- **Strengths**

Our organization has a network of dedicated volunteers with diverse skill sets, including social workers, educators, and community organizers. We have established strong partnerships with local businesses, donors, and government agencies to leverage resources effectively.

- **Problem**

Observing the plight of vulnerable populations in our community, we recognize a pressing need to address poverty, homelessness, and lack of access to basic necessities. We are called to be a beacon of hope for those facing hardships, empowering them to break the cycle of despair.

- **Holy Spirit prompting**

Through prayer and seeking God's guidance, we have felt a clear calling to significantly impact the lives of those in need. The Holy Spirit has prompted us to provide immediate relief and long-term support and resources that will enable individuals and communities to thrive.

Mission Statement: Hope For All exists to bring hope and practical help to those in need, empowering them to build a better future for themselves and their communities.

Hope For All Sample Vision Scope

Mission
"Hope For All exists to bring hope and practical help to those in need, empowering them to build a better future for themselves and their communities."

Values

- **Empowerment**

We believe in empowering individuals and families to take control of their lives and break the cycle of poverty.

- **Education**

We value education as a powerful tool for personal and societal transformation, and we strive to provide access to education for all.

- **Community**

We are committed to building strong and resilient communities through collaboration, mutual support, and shared responsibility.

- **Sustainability**

We seek to create sustainable solutions that address the root causes of poverty and promote long-term positive change.

Past

- **Recent past**

In the past year, Hope For All has expanded its reach to three new cities, doubling its impact on the community. We have also faced a challenge in funding, with a major donor pulling out unexpectedly. However, we were able to pivot and launch a successful crowdfunding campaign to make up the difference.

- **Mid-range past**

Over the past two to four years, Hope For All has developed several new programs to address the root causes of poverty in our community. We have also built strong partnerships with local businesses and government agencies to expand our impact. One major challenge during this time was a leadership transition, which required significant time and resources to ensure a smooth transition.

- **Long-range past**

Hope For All has some significant legacy wins. One of the most impactful was collaborating with other nonprofits to advocate for a change in local housing policy, resulting in more affordable housing options for low-income families. We have also been recognized nationally for our innovative approach to addressing food insecurity, which has been replicated in other communities nationwide.

Vision

- **Long-range vision (5+ years)**

We are a lighthouse of Christ, illuminating the path for the poor and oppressed, guiding them toward a brighter future through compassionate service and advocacy.

Hope For All envisions a world where every individual, regardless of circumstance, has equitable access to life's basic necessities—nutritious food, shelter, education, and healthcare. Our mission is deeply rooted in empowerment, believing in Christ's power to help everyone break free from the cycle of poverty.

Through the transformative power of education, we equip individuals and families with the tools they need to take control of their lives, fostering self-sufficiency and igniting lasting change. We seek to address the root causes of poverty, embracing sustainable solutions that meet immediate needs and lay the foundation for long-term positive transformations.

Bound by our core values, we build resilient communities through a spirit of collaboration, mutual support, and shared responsibility. Guided by our faith in Christ's teachings, we strive to create a world where hope is kindled and the possibilities for growth and personal transformation are limitless.

With innovative programs and strategic partnerships, we work tirelessly to eradicate poverty, inequality, and injustice in the communities we serve. As we spread the love and hope of Christ to all people, our beacon of compassion shines bright, inspiring a collective journey toward a future where everyone can achieve their God-given potential. Together, we strive to build a better, more compassionate world where hope thrives, lives are transformed, and communities flourish.

- **Mid-range milestones (2–4 years)**

Increase partnerships with local churches. Hope For All aims to establish partnerships with a minimum of ten new local churches within the next two to four years. This will be measured by the number of formal collaboration agreements signed and joint events or service projects organized annually.

Expand volunteer base. Hope For All will strive to recruit and retain at least fifty new volunteers annually. Volunteer satisfaction will be assessed through bi-annual surveys, with a target of maintaining an overall satisfaction rating of 90 percent or higher.

Develop spiritual formation programs. Over the next two to four years, Hope For All is dedicated to implementing a minimum of two comprehensive spiritual formation programs. Our aim is to actively engage 60 percent of those we serve in our discipleship program, nurturing their spiritual growth and fostering a deeper connection with faith. Additionally, we aspire to see 50 percent of program participants successfully graduating from our new job preparation training, equipping them with the skills and confidence to thrive in their future careers.

Increase financial sustainability. Hope For All aims to raise an additional $200,000 in grant funding and donations over the next two to four years. The success of fundraising campaigns and social enterprise initiatives will be measured against predefined financial targets, and regular financial reports will be provided to donors and supporters to maintain transparency and trust.

- **One-year battle cry**

"Expanding our reach and impact to serve more people in need."

Primary objectives

- Increase outreach efforts to underserved communities through targeted marketing campaigns and partnerships with local organizations.
- Develop and implement new programs to meet the evolving needs of those experiencing poverty and homelessness.
- Expand partnerships with businesses and foundations to secure additional funding and resources to support the organization's mission.

- Improve volunteer recruitment and training programs to better equip volunteers to meet clients' needs.
- Strengthen data collection and analysis systems to measure services' impact and identify improvement areas.

Distractions: What opportunities are presenting themselves that may be distractions and could get us off course?

- A new funding source has become available but requires significant time and resources to apply for and manage.
- A partnership opportunity with a local community center has arisen, but it would require a significant shift in focus from our current programs.
- Pursuing the new funding source could take time and resources away from other important initiatives, and there is no guarantee of success.
- Shifting the focus to the community center partnership could divert attention and resources from existing programs, potentially causing them to suffer.

Dangers: What are the dangers we need to be aware of as we move forward?

- A sudden economic downturn could result in decreased donations and funding, making it difficult to maintain current programs.
- Changes to government policies or regulations could have a negative impact on our ability to operate or receive funding.

4

Teaching

In 1986, I (Mac) made a financial decision that many would call foolish. I had the option to pay $5,000 or $25,000 for seminary, and I chose the more expensive option to attend Dallas Theological Seminary (DTS). The reason for my decision was simple: I wanted to study under the teachings of Dr. Howard Hendricks.

You see, while doing my undergrad, I had the opportunity to watch a teaching video of Dr. Hendricks, and I was mesmerized by his ability to grab students' attention and motivate them to action. He was the type of teacher I dreamed of becoming. So, when choosing a seminary, I would pay anything to sit under his teachings. Though it was a high price to pay, I can honestly say I never regretted that decision. Dr. Hendricks' impact on my life was priceless.

Great teachers, like Dr. Hendricks, draw you in, educate, challenge, and inspire you, and give you a hunger to change. As a leader, you may not see yourself as a teacher, but you are constantly communicating lessons to your team, staff, or congregation. Unfortunately, many leaders do not see themselves as teachers and therefore do not strive to improve their teaching abilities. This can result in their team members not being challenged or inspired, new leaders not being developed, and congregations not being hungry for growth as disciples.

Jesus, too, was a great teacher. The Gospel writers often described the crowds as being "amazed" when they heard his teaching. The Greek word is *ekplesso,* which means "to be exceedingly struck in mind."[1] Jesus communicated in a way that people could not ignore, and his teachings led people to travel great distances or make great sacrifices to listen to him.

As a leader, you have the opportunity to galvanize people around a significant mission, just like Jesus did. But that won't happen if you leave people bored and uninspired. You are a teacher, whether behind a pulpit, at a boardroom table, or sitting at a café high-top engaging in a one-on-one. And the more you care about your mission, the more you will strive to become a leader who teaches with excellence.

In this module, we are going to focus on the character trait of confidence and the competency of teaching. We will guide you through six practices for becoming an effective teaching leader. By the end of this module, you'll be equipped with the tools and knowledge to teach and inspire those around you, just like Jesus did.

First, let's define our terms:

Character: *Confidence*
Leaders fully trust in the guidance of the Holy Spirit, enabling them to approach challenges and decisions with self-assurance and peace.

Competency: *Teaching*
Impart knowledge, skills, and values to learners, inspiring and motivating them to actively engage in personal and spiritual growth.

Objectives

1. Recognize ways to cultivate and strengthen your God-confidence.
2. Evaluate how effectively you integrate the principles and truths you teach others into your own life.
3. Commit to adequate preparation, ongoing research, and study to improve your teaching skills.
4. Discover the importance of utilizing diverse teaching techniques to engage your audience and effectively deliver your message.
5. Practice evaluating your communication skills and seek constructive feedback from others to enhance your teaching abilities.

Deepen Your Character: *Confidence*

When I (Mac) started preaching regularly in 1990, I thought I had it all figured out. I had taken preaching classes, taught at youth group, and read a lot of books to help sharpen my communication skills. But after a couple of months of regularly speaking to adults, I started to feel insecure about my teaching. It didn't take long for me to develop a sense of inadequacy when, week after week, I saw people fall asleep or appear bored during my messages.

My insecurity hit a new level when I overheard someone criticizing my teaching—I was devastated. Feeling like a failure, I began to wonder if I was cut out for this kind of work. I began to doubt myself and my abilities as a communicator and teacher.

It took years for God to work on my soul and show me that I was not teaching to please or impress people. I was simply a vessel in his hands, and my job was to listen to what he wanted me to say, study the best I could, and deliver the message he assigned to me.

It wasn't an easy journey, but I found my own teaching voice over time. Even more importantly, I developed a God-confidence that prevented me from seeking approval and to instead trust in my identity in Christ for my confidence.

As I reflect on that journey, I realize that confidence is a character trait that every leader needs. But not just any kind of confidence; we need God-confidence. It's the confidence Jesus displayed in his Father. In John 8:28, Jesus says, "I do nothing on my own but speak just what the Father has taught me." He only taught what he received from the Father.

As we strive to become better teachers, we can learn from Jesus' example and seek to find our confidence in God, not in our own wisdom or intellect as teachers. Proverbs 3:5–6 tells us, "Trust in the Lord with all your heart and lean not on your own understanding; in all your ways submit to him, and he will make your paths straight."

Developing God-confidence as a communicator and teacher is not something that happens overnight. It's a process that requires us to surrender our fears and doubts to God and trust him to guide us. When we are confident in our identity in Christ, we can speak boldly and with authority, knowing that we are not speaking on our own behalf but on behalf of the one who has called us. We must remember the power is not in our words but in the Spirit of God speaking through the Word of God itself.

So, as you embark on your own journey as a teaching leader, remember that you are not alone. God is with you every step of the way, guiding you and giving you the confidence you need to share his message with others.

Scripture

As you read the following Scripture, meditate on what the author wishes to communicate and answer the questions below. Allow the Holy Spirit to speak to you and challenge you as a leader about how you can develop your character so that you can grow in confidence in your everyday life.

Proverbs 3:5-6

Trust in the LORD with all your heart and lean not on your own understanding; in all your ways submit to him, and he will make your paths straight.

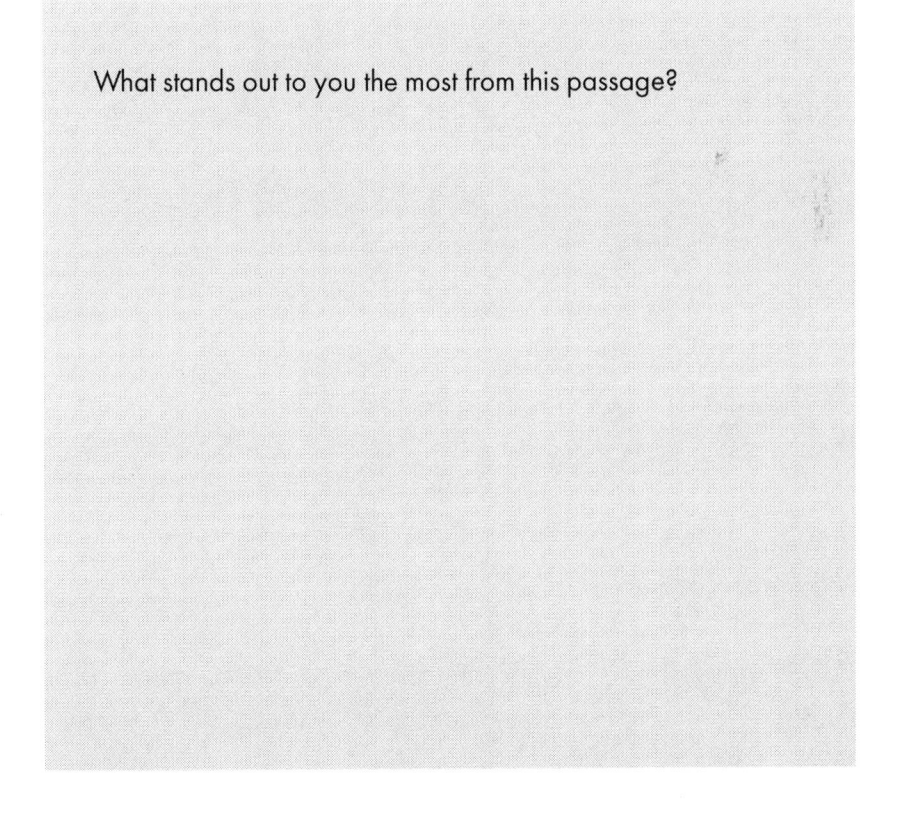

What stands out to you the most from this passage?

> In what area of your teaching or preaching do you find it most challenging to trust in the Lord rather than relying on your own understanding?
>
> What steps can you take to cultivate God-confidence in your role as a teaching leader?

Now that we have examined the character trait of confidence, we can begin working through the core competency for this module: *teaching*. As you read what follows, note how confidence can undergird a leader's competency in teaching.

Develop Your Competency: *Teaching*
Preassessment

Before proceeding, complete the assessment below. In the final module of this training guide, you will retake it as a postassessment to measure your transformation and growth in this competency.

The following proficiencies demonstrate mastery of this module's competency. For each of them, give yourself a grade of A, B, C, D, or E to reflect your actual level of competency today. Giving yourself an A+ indicates you are a model for others to follow. An E indicates no mastery.

Proficiency	Preassessment
I regularly apply the teachings I share to my own life and strive to be a living example of the message I deliver to others.	
I utilize various teaching techniques in my sermons and lessons to cater to people's short attention spans and make the message more engaging.	
I devote sufficient time to preparing and studying before delivering my teaching.	
I invest time researching and studying effective teaching methods to continually grow and improve as a teacher.	
I regularly evaluate my communication skills and seek feedback from others to improve my teaching abilities.	

Which of the five proficiencies do you want to grow in the most? Why is it important for you to grow in that aspect?

What did you learn about your teaching style and methods from taking this assessment?

Were there any surprises or areas that you identified as needing improvement?

What is the most important next step you need to take to grow as a teaching leader?

Six Practices of a Teaching Leader

I (Mac) knew my boss, John, cared about me and my success. He was a kind and caring leader who wanted to see each of his company's twelve real estate agents reach their full potential. As a twenty-five-year-old first-year agent without much experience or credibility, I was grateful to have him as a mentor. He took the time to get to know me, my background, strengths and weaknesses, and my skills and abilities (or should I say my lack of ability!).

What I didn't realize at the time was that John was also a teacher. His stories, experience, client interactions, and staff meetings taught me valuable lessons. He would often have me jump in the car with him to ride around to look at properties. As soon as we got in, he would turn on his Zig Ziglar sales training tapes. He would stop the tape every few minutes, and he would process his learning with me. John understood he had the opportunity to shape the future of those under his leadership and maximized that opportunity by consistently teaching and leading us.

As a leader, it's important to remember that teaching doesn't always have to happen in a traditional classroom setting. The Latin root of the word "education," *educatio*, means "breeding, bringing up, rearing" and comes from the verb *ēducō*, which means "I train." But it also relates to *ēdūcō*, meaning "I lead forth," from the verb *dūcō*, meaning "I lead."[2] This shows that leadership and teaching go hand in hand. As a leader, if you see yourself as a lead teacher and consistently put effort into teaching and developing your team, you can maximize their potential and see them achieve great things.

Now, let's look at six practices for becoming an effective teaching leader.

Practice #1: Define Your Goal

When I (Mac) was in seminary, Dr. Hendricks told us about his experience as a guest speaker at a church. As he walked into the pulpit, he couldn't help but notice a note taped to the top of the podium that read, "What are you trying to do to these people?" The note caught him off guard and left him feeling a bit uneasy. After the service, he asked the pastor about it, and the response he received was unexpected.

The pastor told him that he had been preaching "just to preach" for years. He would share information about Scripture without any real emphasis on how it could be applied to people's lives. But then, one day, he had an epiphany. He realized his sermons were not just about imparting knowledge but also, and more importantly, about transforming people's lives and helping them live like Jesus.

This story is a powerful reminder that the goal of teaching is not just about dispensing information but about transforming lives. As a young leader, I, too, struggled with how to help people grow. But through much reflection and experience, I have developed a framework that has proven extremely effective in producing transformation in learners. I call it the triad of development.

The triad includes three overlapping elements that work together to produce transformation in our learners: knowledge, experience, and coaching. In fact, if you recall, it's this triad that undergirds the philosophy for this training guide. (See pages xii–xiv.)

First up, we have *knowledge*. This is where we equip learners with vital information and insights related to the specific skills they want to develop. Let us illustrate. Imagine you're teaching someone public speaking skills; you'd guide them to explore valuable resources, such as books on presentation techniques or dedicated videos on public speaking.

But remember, knowledge alone won't cut it; we need more to improve their speaking abilities. That's where *experience* comes into play as the second element. True transformation happens when learners put their newfound knowledge into action. It's all about practical application that really accelerates growth. When they face challenges and learn from both successes and failures, they gain a deeper understanding of the subject matter. Every time they successfully execute a skill, their confidence and grasp of leadership significantly improve.

Now, let's stick with the public speaking example. After they've read and gained knowledge about public speaking, you'd aim to challenge them with various speaking tasks to practice. You would give them opportunities for gradual improvement through ongoing practice, bit by bit. You'd also give them practical assignments, such as writing an introduction to a talk, leading a devotional for the team, or even letting them share a portion of a training session you are leading.

Lastly, we have *coaching*, the third and final aspect of the triad. Here's where you observe your learners in action, providing constructive feedback, and having discussions about their progress.

So, with public speaking, you'd actually watch them deliver a speech and them give feedback on their presentation style and content. You'd coach them on details such as vocal tone, pacing, and body language, which further refine their skills. This coaching phase solidifies their learning, helping them internalize and apply feedback effectively. The assignments given during this stage lead to more practice, nurturing further growth.

When you consistently practice all three elements of the triad, studies have shown that people are more likely to improve their skills and achieve their goals. Combining knowledge, experience, and coaching is key to achieving transformation and success in learning. In fact, a study conducted by Olivero, Bane, and Kopelman in 1997 found that training alone increased productivity by 22.4 percent, while training combined with coaching increased productivity by 88 percent.[3]

The triad of development is a powerful tool to transform learners, combining knowledge, experiential learning, and personalized coaching to unlock their full potential. This framework will help you effectively teach and produce transformative results in others.

Practice #2: Live Out the Truth You Teach

The people who listen to you regularly teach want to know that you are a person who walks closely with Christ. They know you're not perfect. But they need to know that you are pursuing God's heart. King David was imperfect, but his faithful followers knew he was a man after God's heart.

Your character matters when it comes to being a trusted communicator of God's truth. If the people don't perceive that their leader is being transformed, they will tune out.

The recent story of Will Smith and Chris Rock at the 2022 Academy Awards ceremony perfectly illustrates this concept. When Chris Rock hurled a poorly crafted comedic insult at Will Smith's wife, Smith walked onto the stage and slapped him. Minutes later, Smith won the Oscar for Best Actor and gave an acceptance speech that could have been profound and powerful. He said, "I am overwhelmed by what God is calling on me to do and be in this world … I want to be a vessel for love."[4] But after the slap, the words fell to the ground, and his credibility was damaged.

The lesson here is clear: who you are speaks so loudly that others can't hear what you say. As a teacher, you must seek to live the life you invite others to live. This is what gives you credibility with your people. With each lesson you teach, people must sense that the truth you are teaching is the truth you live.

So, as you prepare a training lesson, devotional, or sermon, look for a particular point of application for your own life. Be specific about a step of obedience that God wants you to take based on the truth you intend to proclaim. In other words, practice what you preach *before* you preach. Put on your SPECS as you study: in the text, is there a *Sin* to avoid, a *Promise* to claim, an *Example* to follow, a *Command* to obey, or a *Service* to perform?

Live out the truths you will be teaching. Even if you can only do so a day or two before the message, put into practice the practical ideas you will be sharing with your listeners. This calls for integrity and authenticity. You can share how helpful and difficult it has been to put these principles into practice in your own life.

As you seek to regularly make applications of the truths you are teaching, you will be growing in your godly character. You will be pursuing holiness. Often, you can share with those you are leading how God has challenged and changed you in a particular way. As you increasingly become conformed to the image of Christ, your teaching will become more credible and more powerful.

> On a scale of 1–5, how often do you intentionally live out the truths you teach in your personal life and leadership?

> What obstacles or challenges do you encounter in integrating these truths into your life? What steps can you take to ensure you consistently model the truths you teach?

Practice #3: Prepare Your Mind

In my mid-twenties, one of my (Mac) mentors taught me a communication lesson I've never forgotten. Pastor David Joyner, coaching me on preaching, pointed to the pulpit and said, "Mac, as a young man, I walked into that pulpit unprepared once in my life. That day I didn't steward God's Word with integrity or responsibility. God broke my heart as he revealed my laziness in preparation. So from that day, I committed to God that I would never again stand behind that holy desk unprepared."

That commitment made him one of the greatest preachers I've ever heard. The phrase "holy desk" was forever etched in my mind—giving me a holy fear of my responsibility to teach God's Word with truth and passion.

Prayer and preparation put God's power in the message. Preparation includes preparing our soul, mind, and content. Preparation is key to delivering a powerful message that impacts your audience. However, the way you prepare will be unique to you. So here are a few tips to help you cultivate a prepared mind.

- **Talk to other communicators about how they prepare**

Ask other communicators how long they take to prepare, what hacks they have discovered, what their research process and teaching outline looks like. Ask how they prepare their soul, mind, and content. Although we all have a unique communication style, learning best practices and transferable concepts from others is helpful.

- **Constantly collect ideas and illustrations**

Rick Warren says,

> I am a collector of ideas, collecting future sermon series and ideas. There are some series I've been collecting for 20 years that I still haven't preached on. For instance, I did a series through Psalm 23 a few years ago. I have collected material for more than 20 years. I just knew that one day I was going to preach on Psalm 23. So when I get a quiet-time insight, when I hear a good sermon and a quote, I throw it in that file. When I get ready to plan a series, I'm not starting from scratch. I have what I call my bucket file. My bucket file is not really organized. It is just stuff tossed in there. Once you get enough to start making a series, you say to yourself, "I want to do this series on the family, or I want to do this series on I Peter, or I want to do this series on the second coming"—you start the file. Right now, I have maybe 50 series in the hopper.[5]

Start the habit of finding and filing today. Years from now, the payoff will be huge.

- **Create a reusable teaching template**

Are you tired of starting your training lessons or sermons with a blank sheet of paper each time? Trust us, we know the struggle. But guess what? We found a solution that will save you a ton of time: a reusable template.

Your brain craves structure. So, as you prepare a devotion, sermon, or training session for your staff, your brain appreciates the jump start a template offers and can begin filling in the pieces with relevant content instead of trying to figure out a new framework every time. This lets you capture and organize your content more quickly as you prepare.

In his book *Communicating for a Change*, Andy Stanley shares a template he has used for years: Me-We-God-You-We.[6] This template consists of five words and allows you to structure a sermon quickly.

Here's how it works:

Me. Start by sharing a dilemma you have faced or are currently facing. This orients the audience to the topic and lets them know that you see yourself as someone who needs to grow in this area.

We. Next, find common ground with your audience around the same or a similar dilemma. "We" invites the audience to go on a journey with you.

God. Transition to the biblical text to discover what God says about the tension or question you've introduced. Spend most of your message time here, and show how God gives a new perspective and shines fresh light on the tension you raised in the "Me–We" sections.

You. Highlight specific applications and challenge your audience to act on what they have just heard. Think about people's life situations within your audience and make the application so that people will think, "He or she is talking to me."

We. Finally, close your message with several inspirational statements about what God could do in your community, your church, or the world if everyone listening forsook their sin, embraced the truth, followed the Lord, and obeyed his commands.

Of course, you don't have to use this template, but it's a good example as you consider what teaching template you prefer. Having a reusable framework to construct your lessons will save time and allow you to capture and organize your content more quickly. Remember, your brain craves structure, so give it what it wants!

> Think of an experienced communicator you can speak with to learn about their preparation practices. What specific questions will you ask them to gain insights into their process?

> How can you better prioritize preparation time in your schedule to ensure you are adequately prepared for upcoming presentations or training?

What are your thoughts and feelings about incorporating the practice of collecting illustrations into your weekly routine? What benefits do you think it could bring to your communication style?

Practice #4: Employ Diverse Teaching Techniques

Jesus was a master at using diverse teaching techniques. As a rabbi, he employed a range of methods, such as parables, proverbs, questions, dialogue, and hyperbole, to convey complex theological concepts. By utilizing these methods, Jesus engaged with his audience on a deeper level and ensured his message was accessible and resonated with a variety of people.

Research has shown that long lectures are not as effective as using various techniques to maintain engagement and retention.[7] Despite this, many teachers and preachers still choose to use lectures as a primary means of teaching. As a leader, you can use a variety of training techniques when preaching, teaching, or training, all of which will help reach people with diverse learning styles and abilities. Leaders are teachers, and great teachers use various techniques to communicate their message effectively. Keep in mind that the techniques we share below can be used in many different settings, including staff meetings, coaching sessions, or impromptu conversations.

- **Strategic narrative**

This is storytelling presented for a strategic reason in a strategic way. The trainer should intentionally integrate two to four stories in each session. The stories describe a real-life experience from which the trainees can learn. Each story is told in such a way as to capture attention, engage emotions, and inspire new thinking. Strategic narrative paints a picture in the imagination of the listeners and helps them "see" lessons through someone else's experience.

- **Field expert interview**

This involves conducting five- to twenty-minute segments where you, as the teacher, interview someone with significant experience in the topic being taught. Ask pre-selected questions designed to draw from the individual's wisdom and expertise. The audience has the opportunity to learn from the expert's insights and real-world experiences. Additionally, the audience can be invited to ask their own questions, creating an interactive and engaging learning experience. By tapping into the knowledge of those with extensive experience, this approach enriches the learning process and provides valuable, practical knowledge to the learners.

- **Directive teaching**

This teaching technique involves delivering short, focused segments where the facilitator imparts valuable information, facts, and practical steps related to the specific competency being addressed in the session. It takes the form of a brief, insightful presentation aimed at helping the audience gain deeper insights into the subject matter.

For example, it could be a session titled "Three Reasons Why Jesus Traveled Through Samaria" or "Four Tips for Delegating Tasks."

During a directive teaching segment, the audience plays a passive role, actively listening as the teacher or trainer presents important information. These segments serve as a means of summarizing and concentrating the learning, providing a clear and practical application of the concepts being taught. By delivering meaningful content in a concise format, this approach maximizes the impact of the learning experience, ensuring that participants gain valuable knowledge and skills relevant to the session's objectives.

- **Demonstration**

The expertise of the facilitator or a guest presenter is used to show how an activity is done with proficiency. This live model gives the trainees insights into various components of the competency. Typically, the trainees will attempt the skill following the demonstration.

Here are a couple of examples of the demonstration technique.

How to pray Scripture. The facilitator demonstrates a live prayer session, where they skillfully pray using a specific Scripture passage. They showcase how to incorporate the passage into the prayer, reflecting on its significance and applying it to personal situations. Trainees observe the demonstration, and then practice praying Scripture themselves.

How to have a difficult conversation. In this example, the teacher demonstrates how to handle a difficult conversation with empathy and effectiveness. They illustrate active listening, asking open-ended questions, and expressing emotions constructively. Trainees observe the demonstration and debrief afterward to summarize what they learned.

In both these examples, the demonstration technique offers tangible and practical models for trainees to follow. By witnessing the facilitator's expertise, participants gain valuable insights and a clear understanding of how to apply the demonstrated skills in their own lives.

- **Brainstorming**

The facilitator gathers spontaneous input from participants to build a list of ideas, solutions, or concepts. Mulling over ideas together is intended to stir thinking and generate a discovery level of learning.

- **Guided debrief**

This provides an opportunity for trainees to verbally process and discuss their insights and learnings from a preassigned reading or activity. This exercise fosters meaningful peer interaction, enabling participants to gain further insights and real-world application of the concepts. The engagement level is notably high, as learners are challenged to think critically and draw from their prior knowledge and experiences.

- **Self-assessment**

In this exercise, learners are empowered to evaluate their own skill level or experience in relation to the specific competency covered in the session. By raising self-awareness, it heightens the learners' perceived need for growth and improvement. The facilitator then uses debrief questions to help participants extract personal insights from the exercise. This technique not only aids learners in gauging their abilities but also provides the trainer with valuable insights into each learner's skill level.

- **Design analysis**

This involves presenting a sample of something (e.g., a writing sample, artwork, or marketing copy) to the trainees and engaging them in a thorough analysis of its various components. This exercise allows students to examine the work of an expert, understanding what makes it effective and impactful. It also encourages active participation, as trainees can ask questions and explore possibilities for redesigning their own work or gaining new insights into a specific skill.

- **Scenario**

This technique uses case studies/stories to help the learner process a situation they may face. The characters in the scenario exhibit certain leadership behaviors (either positive or negative examples). Debrief questions help the learners process the situation and how it relates to their specific situation. This narrative learning style is intended to help the learners think in a detailed way about their leadership context. Download a sample at www.multiplygroup.org/leadinganorganization.

- **Strategy development**

Participants are prompted to actively process and outline the action steps they will take in response to the training session. This valuable exercise is ideally integrated at any point during the lesson, allowing five to fifteen minutes for learners to contemplate and plan specific applications of the concepts they've learned.

By engaging in strategy development, participants are encouraged to design actionable outcomes that become integral components of their personalized plans. This exercise sparks the highest level of engagement and practical application for trainees, empowering them to take ownership of their learning and apply it to real-life scenarios.

Following the exercise, a debriefing session is conducted, providing an opportunity for learners to share their action steps and verbalize their plans. This fosters a sense of accountability and enables participants to gain additional insights from their peers' strategies and further refine their own approaches.

- **Practice**

This allows the learner to use the competency or an aspect of the skill they've been learning. Sometimes they practice as individuals; other times, the whole class practices the competency together. The intent is to help the learner assess and make specific applications to improve in the particular competency.

Now that you have learned these eleven teaching techniques, start experimenting with them.

For example, try using different techniques in your next thirty-five-minute sermon to engage your audience more deeply. It might look something like this:

Strategic narrative: 5 minutes
Brainstorm: 6 minutes
Directive teaching: 12 minutes
Self-assessment: 4 minutes
Directive teaching: 8 minutes

Or, in your next staff training, try an outline like this:

Brainstorm: 10 minutes
Directive teaching (show a short video): 8 minutes
Guided debrief (what stood out from that video?): 12 minutes
Strategy design (discuss how each person will apply what they learned): 10 minutes

Using various techniques may be intimidating if you are only accustomed to a lecture-based style. But give it a try, evaluate it, and grow as you expand your use of teaching techniques. Over time you will discover that your audience appreciates it and grows more as a result.

Practice #5: Embrace Continuous Growth

Over the years, I (Mac) have had extensive experience teaching content on the leadership pipeline. But on one particular day three years ago I knew I was in trouble as a teacher. As I drove home after teaching on the leadership pipeline for six hours, the thought hit me: *I did not say anything today that I have not said before.* Had I stopped learning about leadership development? Was I growing stale? On my drive home, I confessed to God that I had grown lazy in learning more about leadership development. So that evening, I said, "Ok, God, I have studied leadership development more than anyone I know, and I am at a 401 level of knowledge. But, starting today, my 401 level is my new 101 level. So, that means I need to spend the next few years asking questions I've never asked, reading things I've never read, exposing myself to people I have not been exposed to in order to grow to a new 401 level."

It's easy to stop growing as a communicator. We get comfortable with our existing level of proficiency. But we must recognize there is still untapped potential inside each of us to grow as communicators.

Maybe you consider yourself at an actual 101 level. Or maybe you have a little experience and consider yourself at the 201 level. For some, you may have been teaching for years and consider yourself at a 401 level of proficiency. No matter your level, we urge you to commit to never stop growing as a communicator. Teaching the truths of God is too important to settle for mediocrity.

What is your greatest strength as a teacher? How could you grow that strength to the next level?

Practice #6: Regularly Evaluate Your Effectiveness

When asked to name the three most essential components of rhetoric, Demosthenes, a Greek statesman and orator in ancient Athens, reportedly said, "Delivery, delivery, delivery." As Christians, we can't agree with him. We might say, "God, God, God" or "Truth, truth, truth." But Demosthenes' answer highlights just how important delivery is.

Wouldn't you love to have heard Jesus teach in person? Surely, his delivery was magnificent, and, as we have explored, he "taught as one who had authority" (Matthew 7:29).

If your content is great, but your delivery is poor, your listeners will become disengaged. So, wise teachers will seek continuous improvement in what they say and how they say it.

You might want to study a few of your favorite preachers or teachers who keep you engaged. Consider the following aspects of delivery:

- Use pauses effectively
- Make eye contact
- Vary the pitch, pace, and volume
- Be conversational
- Speak confidently
- Make gestures
- Be yourself
- Articulate clearly
- Avoid verbal fillers like "um," "uh," "you know," and "like"
- Leverage facial expressions

Before you speak, practice out loud! Speak through your notes at least once. Have a stopwatch running. Have a pencil or pen in hand. Delete things that distract. Add clarifying transitions and explanations. Delete unnecessary words and phrases. Tweak. Strengthen. Cut out the weakest ideas that are putting you over your time limit. Practice your delivery. When will you speak faster, slower, more loudly, or more softly? What will you do with your face, hands, and body? How will you express your passion? As you end your rehearsal, pray for yourself and your listeners.

You'll never improve as a teacher if you aren't intentional about evaluation. Build a team of trusted people—people you know are for you—who can give you feedback about content and delivery.

When you meet with your team to evaluate your preaching, it's important to avoid falling into the trap of mutual admiration. Although positive feedback is valuable, it's equally important to receive honest feedback highlighting improvement areas. If your evaluation meetings are becoming predictable and lackluster, it's time to shake things up.

To encourage more thoughtful and constructive feedback,

consider crafting specific questions that challenge your team to think critically about your message.

One effective method for evaluating the messages of a preaching team is the Keep-Start-Stop approach, as shared by a pastor friend of ours. Each week, the team gathers to provide feedback to the speaker, using the following process:

- **Keep**

The team highlights a specific aspect of the message that the speaker executed well and should continue to incorporate into future presentations. This positive reinforcement encourages the speaker to maintain their strengths.

- **Start**

The team identifies any elements or points that were missing from the message and could have enhanced its impact. This constructive feedback guides the speaker to consider new ideas and angles for improvement.

- **Stop**

The team points out any distracting or ineffective elements in the communicator's delivery or content. This feedback helps the speaker to be aware of potential shortcomings and to avoid such distractions in future presentations.

By following the Keep-Start-Stop framework, your team can cultivate a culture of open and honest feedback, enabling speakers to continually refine their messages and enhance their effectiveness. This approach nurtures growth and development within the team, ultimately leading to more impactful and engaging presentations.

No matter what approach you use, evaluating your lesson's effectiveness is important. So at a minimum, consider asking your team for one or two specific suggestions on how to improve. Some potential areas to focus on include:

- Adding energy to the lesson
- Improving the flow of the lesson
- Increasing creativity in the lesson
- Focusing the lesson on a specific topic
- Clarifying confusing points
- Emphasizing the main idea of the lesson
- Making the lesson more practical and applicable

By focusing on specific areas for improvement and gathering targeted feedback, you can receive thoughtful and honest suggestions for enhancing your preaching and making it more effective. This approach can help ensure you receive constructive feedback rather than just generic praise.

Over time you'll be glad you asked for honest critique. And in your heart, you know your people will be as well!

> Describe an approach to message evaluation you would enjoy and benefit from the most.

Conclusion

Being a teaching leader requires intentional effort and commitment. It involves creating a culture of learning and growth within the organization, where teaching and learning are not confined to a pulpit or a classroom but are integrated into everyday interactions.

The six practices outlined in this module provide a framework for leaders to become effective teachers in any setting. By consistently implementing these practices, leaders can inspire and equip those around them to grow and develop, creating a thriving and dynamic organization. As you embark on your journey to becoming a teaching leader, remember that teaching is not just about imparting knowledge but also about modeling and empowering others to learn and grow.

> **Put It Into Practice**
>
> Developing a new skill requires practice. Before you get together with your trainer, complete a few of the following assignments to help you grow in your ability to teach.
>
> 1. Put together and deliver a ten-minute devotion or a full sermon using Andy Stanley's Me-We-God-You-Us outline. Ask your trainer and others to give feedback on what you did well and what you could do to grow as a communicator.

2. Observe a preacher/teacher you admire, and take note of the teaching style and delivery of the instructor. Share what you learn with your trainer.

3. Structure and deliver a training session using some of the techniques you learned in this module. Get feedback from your trainer.

4. Read a book on preaching or teaching and go through it with a friend or your trainer. Here are a few recommendations:
    - Dr. Howard Hendricks, *Teaching to Change Lives: Seven Proven Ways to Make Your Teaching Come Alive*
    - Timothy Keller, *Preaching: Communicating Faith in an Age of Skepticism*

- Haddon W. Robinson, *Biblical Preaching: The Development and Delivery of Expository Messages*
- Andy Stanley and Lane Jones, *Communicating for a Change: Seven Keys to Irresistible Communication*
- Bruce Wilkinson, *The Seven Laws of the Learner: How to Teach Almost Anything to Practically Anyone*

5. Interview a communicator and ask the following questions:
    - Tell me about your preparation process.
    - How do you engage your audience?
    - How do you evaluate your own performance?
    - What advice would you give to someone just starting out as a communicator?

Reflect on Your Learning

Where did you grow the most in this competency?

What next step do you need to take to continue to grow in this competency?

Meet With Your Trainer

Consistent practice can be a great beginning to sharpening a skill, but developing a skill also requires processing what you learned with others.

Meet with your trainer and discuss what you learned from this module.

Dig Deeper

If you are leading or participating in an internship or want to continue to grow in the competency of teaching, go to https://www.multiplygroup.org/internship-planner to download the companion guide to this book.

1. "Greek Word Studies: Astonished (1605) ekplesso," sermonindex.net, https://www.sermonindex.net/modules/articles/index.php?view=article&aid=33555. See, for example, "And when Jesus finished these sayings, the crowds were astonished [*ekplesso*] at his teaching, for he was teaching them as one who had authority, and not as their scribes" (Matthew 7:28–29 ESV); "And they were astonished [*ekplesso*] at his teaching, for he taught them as one who had authority, and not as the scribes" (Mark 1:22 ESV); "And on the Sabbath he began to teach in the synagogue, and many who heard him were astonished [*ekplesso*], saying, 'Where did this man get these things? What is the wisdom given to him? How are such mighty works done by his hands?'" (Mark 6:2 ESV).

2. "Education," https://www.yourdictionary.com/education; "Ducere," https://en.wiktionary.org/wiki/ducere.

3. Denise K. Bane, Richard E. Kopelman, and Gerald Olivero, "Executive Coaching as a Transfer of Training Tool: Effects on Productivity in a Public Agency," *Public Personnel Management* 26, no. 4 (December 1997), https://www.researchgate.net/publication/279449781.

4. Claudia Koerner, "Will Smith Talked About Being A 'Vessel For Love' After Smacking Chris Rock And Winning Best Actor," *Buzzfeed News*, March 28, 2022, https://www.buzzfeednews.com/article/claudiakoerner/will-smith-speech-oscars-apology-smack-chris-rock.

5. "Purpose-Driven Preaching: An Interview with Rick Warren," *Biblia*, accessed September 8, 2023, https://www.biblia.work/sermons/purpose-driven-preaching-an-interview-with-rick-warren/.

6. Andy Stanley and Lane Jones, *Communicating for a Change: Seven Keys to Irresistible Communication* (Colorado Springs, CO: Multnomah, 2006), chapter thirteen.

7. Aleszu Bajak, "Lectures aren't just boring, they're ineffective, too, study finds," *Science*, May 12, 2014, https://www.science.org/content/article/lectures-arent-just-boring-theyre-ineffective-too-study-finds.

5

Financial Stewardship

In the early 1990s, financial consultant Dave Ramsey was living the American Dream. He had built a real estate empire worth over $4 million and was living the high life. But behind the scenes, he struggled with mounting debt and financial stress.

When the real estate market crashed, Ramsey's world came crashing down with it. He found himself bankrupt and with over $1 million in debt. He had to sell everything he owned, including his beloved home and cars, just to stay afloat. He was devastated and felt like a failure.

Ramsey knew he had to do something to turn his life around. He began to study everything he could about personal finance and debt reduction. He poured over the Bible and other financial resources and created a plan to get out of debt and start living within his means.

The journey was long and difficult. Ramsey had to make painful sacrifices, cut back on expenses, and work long hours to rebuild his career. But he persisted, driven by a deep desire to be a good steward of the resources God had entrusted to him.

Through hard work, discipline, and obedience to the principles of biblical stewardship, Ramsey was able to pay off his debts and start a new career as a financial counselor and educator. He wrote books, started hosting a radio show, and created financial courses that have helped millions of people to get out of debt, build wealth, and live more fulfilling lives.

Ramsey's story is a powerful testament to the importance of financial stewardship. He knows firsthand the emotional toll that debt and financial mismanagement can cause when you lead an organization. Still, he also knows the freedom and opportunity that come with being a wise and faithful steward of the resources God entrusts to us.

As Dave Ramsey calls it, paying "stupid tax" can be a painful and expensive lesson to learn, and organizational leaders are not immune to its consequences. By committing to sound financial practices, you can avoid the costly consequences of "stupid tax" and achieve long-term success as you steward your organization's finances.

Let's be real. We've all made some financial mistakes in our lives, and as leaders, we're not immune to them either. In fact, the two of us have seen some pretty common mistakes that can cripple an organization's finances, and we've even made a few ourselves.

One of the biggest mistakes we've observed is failing to plan. You know the saying, "Failing to plan is planning to fail." Well, it's true. Without a solid financial plan, you're just winging it and hoping for the best. And that's a surefire way to end up in a financial crisis.

Another mistake is overspending. It's easy to get caught up in the moment and spend money without thinking about the long-term consequences. But overspending can quickly lead to financial trouble, and before you know it, you may have to cut essential areas of your organization or even lay people off.

Some leaders also overlook the importance of accountability when it comes to financial stewardship. It's not just the responsibility of the senior pastor or CEO; the whole team should be involved. If you're not sharing financial updates with your team, they're missing out on valuable lessons and practices that can help keep your organization financially healthy.

And let's not forget about the emotional aspect of financial management. When leaders make decisions based on their emotions or gut feelings, it can lead to inconsistency and bad habits. We've seen this happen, and it's not pretty. It leads to foolish decisions and can cause your team to lose confidence in your leadership.

That's why this module is so important. We'll examine the character trait of generosity and the competency of financial stewardship and explore how these work together. We'll give you five financial practices to help you steward your organization's finances well and avoid costly mistakes.

First, let's define our terms:

Character: *Generosity*
Leaders manage finances guided by biblical principles, enabling them to participate in God's work of transforming lives and communities.

Competency: *Financial Stewardship*
Implement financial strategies that ensure financial sustainability while maintaining transparency, accountability, and compliance with legal and biblical standards.

Objectives

1. Evaluate your generosity in light of biblical principles.
2. Develop a theology of biblical stewardship to guide your organization.

3. Create an annual planning rhythm to align your organization's finances with its mission and vision.
4. Practice creating an annual budget to align your organization's resources with its priorities.
5. Interview and glean financial insights from a leader who is experienced in financial management.

Deepen Your Character:
Generosity

At Cuyahoga Valley Church (CVC), we have been blessed with faithful givers who have enabled us to end each year in good financial health. But as a leader, I (Rick) have seen colleagues in other churches facing financial challenges, and their first instinct is often to focus on encouraging their people to give more.

However, I believe the first question we should ask ourselves is this: "Am I leading by example when it comes to generosity?"

Generosity is a powerful force that can transform lives and communities. In 1 Chronicles 29, King David and his leaders set an inspiring example of generosity. They offered their personal treasures willingly and generously for the building of the Lord's temple, which encouraged others to give freely as well. By modeling this level of sacrificial giving, David and his leaders demonstrated that generosity fuels generosity.

When we practice the joy of generosity in our own lives, we become better equipped to encourage others to do the same. But if we fail to walk the walk of generosity, our words about stewardship may fall on deaf ears. We may be tempted to dilute the biblical message on stewardship to match our own low levels of giving. We may be unable to share personal stories of sacrificial sowing and supernatural reaping. And we may fail to experience the promise that "all these things will be added to you" because we are not seeking God's kingdom first (Matthew 6:33 ESV).

To become better stewards of our resources, we need to cultivate the habit of generosity in our own lives. This means spending time alone with God and praying honestly about our attitudes toward wealth and giving. Generosity is a lifelong process of growth and learning, but as we walk down the path of giving, we will be better equipped to encourage others to do the same. As Jesus said, "The student is not above the teacher, but everyone who is fully trained will be like their teacher" (Luke 6:40).

So we should strive to practice the joy of generosity in our own lives and become the kind of leaders who God can use to transform lives and communities through our faithful stewardship.

Scripture

As you read the following Scripture, meditate on what the author wishes to communicate and answer the questions below. Allow the Holy Spirit to speak to you and challenge you as a leader about how you can develop your character so that you can grow in generosity in your everyday life.

1 Chronicles 29:1-9

Then King David said to the whole assembly: "My son Solomon, the one whom God has chosen, is young and inexperienced. The task is great, because this palatial structure is not for man but for the LORD God. With all my resources I have provided for the temple of my God—gold for the gold work, silver for the silver, bronze for the bronze, iron for the iron and wood for the wood, as well as onyx for the settings, turquoise, stones of various colors, and all kinds of fine stone and marble—all of these in large quantities. Besides, in my devotion to the temple of my God I now give my personal treasures of gold and silver for the temple of my God, over and above everything I have provided for this holy temple: three thousand talents of gold (gold of Ophir) and seven thousand talents of refined silver, for the overlaying of the walls of the buildings, for the gold work and the silver work, and for all the work to be done by the craftsmen. Now, who is willing to consecrate themselves to the LORD today?" Then the leaders of families, the officers of the tribes of Israel, the commanders of thousands and commanders of hundreds, and the officials in charge of the king's work gave willingly. They gave toward the work on the temple of God five thousand talents and ten thousand darics of gold, ten thousand talents of silver, eighteen thousand talents of bronze and a hundred thousand talents of iron. Anyone who had precious stones gave them to the treasury of the temple of the LORD in the custody of Jehiel the Gershonite. The people rejoiced at the willing response of their leaders, for they had given freely and wholeheartedly to the LORD. David the king also rejoiced greatly.

What do you learn from David about generosity in this passage?

In what ways have you recently demonstrated generosity? How can you continue cultivating a spirit of generosity in your life and leadership?

How can you encourage a culture of generosity and joy in giving among your team?

Now that we have examined the character trait of generosity, we can begin to work through the core competency for this module: *financial stewardship*. As you read what follows, note how generosity can undergird a leader's competency of financial stewardship.

Develop Your Competency: *Financial Stewardship*
Preassessment

Before proceeding, complete the assessment below. In the final module of this training guide, you will retake it as a postassessment to measure your transformation and growth in this competency.

The following proficiencies demonstrate mastery of this module's competency. For each of them, give yourself a grade of A, B, C, D, or E to reflect your actual level of competency today. Giving yourself an A+ indicates you are a model for others to follow. An E indicates no mastery.

Proficiency	Preassessment
I model biblical principles of financial stewardship in my personal and professional life.	
I seek to align our organization's financial practices with biblical stewardship principles, including generosity, integrity, and accountability.	
I understand our organization's financial goals, strategies, and metrics and how they support our mission and vision.	
I consistently analyze financial data, identify trends and opportunities, and use that information to inform strategic decisions and prioritize investments.	
I foster a culture of financial responsibility and accountability, promoting understanding and engagement with our financial goals and practices.	

Which of the five proficiencies do you want to grow in the most? Why is it important for you to grow in that aspect?

Which of the five proficiency statements do you feel most confident in? Why?

Which of the five proficiency statements do you feel least confident in? Why?

What steps can you take to improve in the areas where you are least proficient?

Five Practices to Maintain a Financially Healthy Organization

I (Mac) was shocked and terrified the day I was asked to oversee all the campus pastors for the ten multisite campuses at Seacoast Church. It was a huge responsibility, and I was thrilled and honored to have been chosen for the role. There was just one small problem—I had little to no competence or confidence when it came to the financial management responsibility of the role.

Part of my job was to do quarterly budget reviews with each campus pastor to ensure they were staying on target with their budgets. This was a critical part of my role, but the truth was, I had no confidence in my ability. How could I ensure these pastors stayed on track financially when I didn't even understand half of the financial jargon? I knew I had to do something, but I wasn't sure what.

Fortunately, Byron Davis, one of our executive team members, came to my rescue. Byron had previously served as the CEO of Fisher Price Toys and was a financial wizard. Seeing my struggle, he pulled me aside and began to coach me on how to run these meetings. He showed me how to read a balance sheet and explained other essential elements required for me to perform that particular duty.

At first, I was unsure and nervous. I feared I would mess up or make a fool of myself in front of the campus pastors. But Byron was patient and supportive. He did the meetings with me, step-by-step, until I felt confident enough to do them on my own. I no longer felt like an imposter or like I was out of my depth.

Looking back, I am grateful for Byron's guidance and mentorship. Without his help, I might have floundered in my role and not been able to fulfill my responsibilities as well as I did. But because of his help, I was able to grow as a leader and gain the skills and confidence I needed to succeed. And for that, I will always be thankful.

Like me, you may feel that financial stewardship is above your head. So, let's dig in and look at five practices to help you get a better grasp on the financial management of an organization.

Practice #1: Commit to Financial Obedience and Dependence on God

Before we dive into the details of organizational financial management, it's important to recognize that financial obedience and dependence on God are fundamental to effective stewardship. By first applying biblical principles to our personal finances and living a life of obedience and dependence on God, we can create a strong foundation for financial leadership in our organizations.

Growing up in a Christian household, I (Rick) learned from a young age that tithing was a fundamental practice. My father, a pastor, taught me that giving 10 percent of one's earnings to the church was an essential part of one's spiritual journey.

I married Maryanne, who grew up in a family that did not practice tithing, but she agreed to the practice after we got married. During the first six months of our marriage, we struggled financially, but we kept our commitment to tithe 10 percent of our income.

During our first year of marriage, I played minor league baseball in the Minnesota Twins system, and we were sent to play in the California League. After paying moving expenses and our first paycheck being late, our bank account was depleted.

One day, after making security deposits for our rent, water, and gas, we had to decide whether to buy groceries or send our tithe check to our home church. I wanted to delay giving to God and buy the groceries, hoping to make up for the tithe later. But Maryanne read the verses in Proverbs 3:9–10, which say, "Honor the LORD with your wealth, with the firstfruits of all your crops; then your barns will be filled to overflowing, and your vats will brim over with new wine." She wanted to tithe first and trust God to see how he would provide.

I followed Maryanne's lead and wrote the check to the church, even though I was hesitant. Later that afternoon, the team was headed up the valley to play a road game in Fresno. We only had one egg and some oatmeal left to eat. We argued about who should eat the egg, with Maryanne insisting that I should have it for strength for the game. We probably split it in the end, and I went on my way to play the game.

I don't remember anything about that game, but I do remember what happened when we returned. Maryanne met me at the ballpark, and when we got to our apartment, she told me to open the refrigerator. To my surprise, the refrigerator was packed with food! Maryanne explained that while she was out for a walk, some fans of the team spotted her and invited her to dinner. They gave us all their leftovers, which filled our refrigerator.

The next morning, we woke up to a knock on the door. When we opened it, no one was there, but we saw three big bags of produce at our feet. One of the young fans had taken a liking to us and dropped off the produce to welcome us to the community.

It was early in the season, and I was off to a slow start. However, the team had a promotion that if a player hit a double, he would win an 8-inch sandwich from a local sandwich shop. If he hit a triple, he won a 16-inch sandwich. He won a 24-inch sandwich plus a soft drink if he hit a home run. The home run also got him a free steak dinner at a local restaurant like Denny's.

After we wrote that tithe check, I started hitting doubles and home runs for the next week or so. We had no money, but we were chowing down, splitting steak dinners and eating sub sandwiches!

Looking back, I believe God was testing us to see if he could trust us. And because of Maryanne, we passed that test. Giving to God first sets in motion a chain reaction of events that can only be explained by God showing up.

Living a life of faith and generosity is essential, not just for personal growth but also for leadership. When leading an organization, it's crucial to model a spirit of generosity and dependence on God's provision. By living this way, you can inspire others to follow in your footsteps, and together, you can experience the incredible blessings that come from giving first to God. As I learned firsthand, you can't outgive God, and seeking the kingdom of God first will always pay off in the end.

> Have you ever struggled with giving first to God and trusting him to provide? How can you apply the lessons from Rick and Maryanne's experience to your own life?

> Can you think of a time when a leader's generosity inspired you to give more?

Practice #2: Commit to a Foundation of Biblical Financial Stewardship

As leaders of organizations, we all have big dreams and goals, and we know that resources are critical to achieving them. Committing to wise financial stewardship and making those dreams a reality takes a team effort. We have a responsibility to manage God's resources effectively, and that's why we need to build a culture of stewardship that's grounded in the Bible.

At Cuyahoga Valley Church (CVC), we invited an expert facilitator to help us identify four key biblical principles that form the foundation of our Theology of Stewardship. Although it took months of study and discussion, the result was a valuable document we frequently reference for guidance in our decision-making and teaching. Here are the four principles undergirding our Theology of Stewardship:

- **God owns everything and needs nothing**

His kingdom never has a "need." While there may be "unfunded kingdom opportunities," neither God nor his work ever needs anything (Deuteronomy 8:18; Job 41:11; Psalm 24:1; 50:10–12; 89:11; Acts 17:24–25; Romans 11:36; Revelation 4:11).

- **We own nothing and need everything**

We are born into this world with empty hands, and we will leave this world with empty hands. We brought nothing with us into the world, and we will take nothing with us out of the world (1 Timothy 6:7). Therefore, we must recognize that we actually possess nothing, and God owns everything. Our responsibility is to manage his possessions while we are on this planet. We cannot contribute to God's work without him providing us with the resources to do so—life, health, money, time, abilities, opportunities, and so forth. Everything we are and everything we have is a gift from God. We can only return to the Lord what has flowed from him in the first place (Ecclesiastes 5:15; John 3:27; 1 Corinthians 4:7; 1 Timothy 6:7).

- **God is the sole provider of all resources**

He provides all our resources, both tangible and spiritual. He uses the resources entrusted to us to sustain us and advance his kingdom. To fully access God's resources, our first priority and responsibility is to humbly and earnestly seek godly wisdom and wise counsel to ensure our vision aligns with God's vision. What God orders, he pays for. God would not give his people a vision and fail to provide them with the funding to realize it (John 15:7; Philippians 4:19; 1 Timothy 6:17; 2 Peter 1:3).

- **God uses stewards to manage his resources**

God uses stewards to manage his resources and deploys them to sustain and advance his kingdom. Since there is no shortage of kingdom resources, God's people already possess everything necessary to accomplish his vision. We are responsible for what he entrusts to us as stewards, not owners. We must not grip tightly to the things he entrusts to us but seek to hold everything loosely. We simply and responsibly manage the treasures he entrusts to us, never forgetting that any way he directs us to share, save, or spend is his sovereign right. Good stewardship is not just releasing a few dollars here and there to a church. We start by surveying all that God has given us and remember how everything that we have, *everything*, kept or released, should be used in light of eternity. God is not asking us just to share our resources; he is asking us to recognize that all our resources belong to him. He wants us to use what we need and then give the rest away. Learning to recognize and receive his direction is critically important to how well we steward what he has entrusted us. We do that by studying the Bible, being prayerful and Spirit-led, and having a posture of surrender. (See Exodus 36:5; 1 Chronicles 29:9; 1 Corinthians 4:2; 2 Corinthians 8:1–5; 9:8, 11.)

For CVC, this document has proven to be invaluable. Teachers can refer to it and pull from it when teaching on generosity. It's instructive when onboarding new staff and when training existing staff. It helps new members understand their responsibility before the Lord and to his church.

Please don't cut and paste CVC's Theology of Stewardship! The language and emphases likely do not match the culture and DNA of your organization. You must help your leaders wrestle with Scripture and develop unique ways to express your Theology of Stewardship. This is how you will gain greater ownership and develop a tool you will actually use.

If you were to write a Theology of Stewardship to help guide your organization, what two or three core beliefs would you want to include?

Practice #3: Implement a Financial Planning Process that Supports Your Organization's Mission and Vision

As a leader, it's always exciting to dream about the future of our organization and the impact we can make. But we can't forget to plan for the financial aspect of those dreams. That's where an annual financial planning process comes in. It's not just about crunching numbers; it's an opportunity to prayerfully consider how God is leading us in the upcoming year and how we can steward his resources well.

Having a consistent budget planning process in place is crucial for any organization. It ensures that everyone has enough time to assess their financial needs and projections for the upcoming year. It also helps to align each department's spending with the overall vision of the organization. Plus, it gives your governing body ample time to review and pray about the budgets before final approval. Once the budget is approved, it's important to communicate the final budget to the entire team before the fiscal year begins.

The budgeting process is critical, but it's easy for leaders lacking financial confidence to overlook its importance. My (Mac) friend Jernigan Schwent, a church planter at Discover Church in Kansas City, understands the significance of this process and approaches it diligently with his staff.

Jernigan follows an annual, highly intentional financial planning process at Discover Church that ensures the budget is vision-based, not randomly built. He uses a document called Vision-Based Budgeting that he has created to guide the process every year. This practice helps Discover Church ensure that they are stewarding kingdom dollars based on God's vision.

The process includes prayer, planning, evaluation, and discussion to identify the resources needed to execute the church's mission effectively. Jernigan encourages his team to think through essential questions such as why they exist, what they need to do to accomplish their mission, and how they will achieve it. The budget serves as a practical tool to fund the execution of their mission.

If you would like to learn more about Discover Church's Vision-Based Budgeting process, you can download their document at www.multiplygroup.org/leadinganorganization.

In terms of timing, the budget planning process should ideally begin several months before the start of the budget period. For example, if your organization's fiscal year begins on January 1, you may want to start the budget planning process in September or October of the previous year. This will allow sufficient time for gathering data, estimating revenue and expenses, developing and reviewing the budget, and getting necessary approvals.

If you want to build out your financial planning process, below is an outline of the typical steps involved in creating a good budget planning process for your church, nonprofit, or business.

- **Step 1: Establish goals and priorities**

Begin by identifying your organization's goals and priorities for the upcoming budget period. This step involves praying and reviewing the organization's Vision Scope that we talked about in module three. Taking a fresh look at your long-range vision, mid-range milestones, and short-range one-year battle cry is crucial in the financial planning process.

- **Step 2: Gather financial data**

Gather financial data from the previous budget period, including income statements, balance sheets, and cash flow statements. This will help you understand your organization's financial position and identify any areas that need improvement.

- **Step 3: Estimate revenue**

Based on past performance and any anticipated changes, estimate the revenue your organization expects to generate during the upcoming budget period.

- **Step 4: Project expenses**

Project your organization's expenses for the upcoming budget period—taking into account any planned changes or initiatives. Allot ample time for this step because each department of your organization needs time to project what they want to accomplish and how much that will cost.

- **Step 5: Develop the budget**

Develop a draft budget that reflects your organization's one-year battle cry, priority objectives, estimated revenue, and projected expenses.

While the specific budget categories for a church, nonprofit, or business may vary depending on the size and scope of the organization, some common categories include personnel, facilities, administrative, capital, program ministry, and outreach expenses.

If you are running a nonprofit, additional budget categories may include fundraising or governance expenses.

If you are running a business, additional budget categories may include sales and marketing, operations, or research and development expenses.

Again, it's important for the organization to customize its budget categories to reflect its unique needs and priorities. By doing so, you can ensure that the organization's resources are used effectively to achieve its goals and objectives.

■ Step 6: Review and approve the budget

Review the draft budget with key stakeholders, such as board members, staff, and volunteers. Make any necessary revisions. Once the budget is finalized, obtain approval from the appropriate authority (such as the board of directors or elders).

■ Step 7: Implement and monitor the budget

Once the budget is approved, implement it and monitor your organization's financial performance regularly to ensure you are staying on track. Make any necessary adjustments as needed.

■ Step 8: Communicate the budget

Communicate the final budget to your team and stakeholders so everyone is aware of the financial goals and objectives for the upcoming year. It's important to ensure that everyone understands their role in achieving those goals and how their department's spending fits into the bigger picture.

- **Step 9: Track progress**

Set up regular meetings to track progress toward meeting the budget goals. This will allow you to make any necessary adjustments in real time and ensure your team is aware of any changes.

- **Step 10: Review and evaluate**

Review and evaluate your organization's financial performance at the end of the budget period. This will give you insight into what worked well and what areas need improvement for the next budget period. It's also an opportunity to celebrate wins and recognize your team's hard work.

Having a well-planned and intentional financial planning process is crucial for any organization, especially when it comes to aligning your budget with your vision and mission. By following these steps and being intentional with your financial planning, you can ensure that your organization is making the most of the resources God has given you.

> What potential risks do you envision in an organization that doesn't have a detailed, written financial planning process they use each year?

Have you or your organization ever used a vision-based budgeting process? If so, how did it work for you? If not, would you consider implementing one? Why or why not?

Practice #4: Conduct Regular Financial Checkups, and Analyze Your Organization's Financial Health

Assessing the financial health of your organization involves analyzing various financial reports and data. Below are some of the key reports and numbers you should consider.

- **Balance sheet**

A balance sheet is a snapshot of your organization's financial position at a specific point in time. It shows your organization's assets, liabilities, and equity. By reviewing the balance sheet, you can assess your organization's liquidity, leverage, and overall financial health.

Assets are the resources that the organization owns and controls, such as cash, investments, property, equipment, and inventory. Liabilities are the debts and obligations that the organization owes to others, such as loans, accounts payable, and accrued expenses. Equity represents the residual interest in the assets of the organization after liabilities are deducted. It includes items such as retained earnings and contributed capital.

The balance sheet follows a basic accounting equation: assets = liabilities + equity. This means that the total assets of the organization must be equal to the total liabilities and equity.

Here is an example of a balance sheet for a hypothetical nonprofit organization:

Assets

- Cash: $100,000
- Investments: $50,000
- Property and equipment: $250,000
- Other assets: $25,000

Total assets: $425,000

Liabilities

- Accounts payable: $10,000
- Accrued expenses: $5,000
- Short-term loans: $20,000
- Long-term loans: $100,000

Total liabilities: $135,000

Equity

- Retained earnings: $100,000
- Contributed capital: $190,000

Total equity: $290,000
Total liabilities and equity: $425,000

In this example, the organization has total assets of $425,000, including cash, investments, property and equipment, and other assets. The organization also has liabilities of $135,000, including accounts payable, accrued expenses, and loans. Finally, the organization has equity of $290,000, including retained earnings and contributed capital.

By reviewing the balance sheet, leaders of churches, nonprofits, and Christian businesses can better understand their organization's financial position and make informed decisions about resource allocation and future investments.

- **Income statement (profit and loss statement)**

An income statement shows your organization's revenues, expenses, and net income or loss over a specific period of time. You can assess your organization's profitability and financial performance by analyzing the income statement.

The profit and loss (P&L) statement shows the net profit or loss of the organization during the period, which is the difference between the total revenues earned and the total expenses incurred. The statement is important because it provides a snapshot of the organization's financial health and helps leaders make informed decisions about budgeting, investments, and resource allocation.

To illustrate how a P&L statement works, let's say you are the leader of a Christian bookstore. Your P&L statement for the fiscal year ending December 31, 2022 might look something like this:

Revenues

- Sales: $500,000

Cost of goods sold

- Inventory costs: $250,000
- Shipping and handling: $10,000

Gross profit: $240,000

Expenses

- Rent and utilities: $50,000
- Employee salaries: $120,000
- Marketing and advertising: $30,000
- Insurance and legal fees: $10,000
- Depreciation and amortization: $5,000
- Other expenses: $10,000

Total expenses: $225,000
Net profit: $15,000

In this example, the bookstore earned $500,000 in sales revenue but had $260,000 in expenses (including the cost of goods sold), resulting in a gross profit of $240,000. After deducting all other expenses, the net profit for the year was $15,000.

Overall, a P&L statement is a crucial tool for leaders of churches, nonprofits, and Christian businesses to understand their financial performance and make informed decisions about the future.

- **Cash flow statement**

A cash flow statement shows how cash is flowing into and out of your organization. It helps you understand your organization's ability to generate cash, pay bills, and invest in future growth. The cash flow statement is divided into three sections: operating, investing, and financing activities.

Operating activities. This section shows the cash flows generated or used by the organization's primary operations, such as revenue from sales, payments to suppliers, and wages paid to employees.

Investing activities. This section shows the cash flows generated or used by the organization's investments in long-term assets, such as property, equipment, or stocks.

Financing activities. This section shows the cash flows generated or used by the organization's financing activities, such as borrowing or repaying loans, issuing or repurchasing shares, or paying dividends.

Here is an example of a cash flow statement for a hypothetical nonprofit organization:

Operating Activities

- Cash received from donations: $100,000
- Cash received from grants: $50,000
- Cash paid to suppliers: -$30,000
- Cash paid to employees: -$50,000

Net cash provided by operating activities: $70,000

Investing Activities

- Cash used to purchase property: -$50,000
- Cash used to purchase equipment: -$20,000

Net cash used in investing activities: -$70,000

Financing Activities

- Cash received from long-term loans: $100,000
- Cash used to repay short-term loans: -$20,000

Net cash provided by financing activities: $80,000
Net increase in cash: $80,000

In this example, the organization had a net increase in cash of $80,000 during the period covered by the cash flow statement. The organization generated cash through operating activities such as donations and grants and used cash to invest in property and equipment. The organization also received cash from long-term loans and used cash to repay short-term loans.

By reviewing the cash flow statement, leaders of churches, nonprofits, and Christian businesses can better understand their organization's ability to generate cash, pay bills, and invest in future growth.

A cash flow statement for a church would look similar to the example above but with different line items that reflect the church's sources and uses of cash. Here's an example of what a cash flow statement for a church might look like:

Operating Activities

- Cash received from tithes and offerings: $150,000
- Cash received from other donations: $10,000
- Cash paid for salaries and benefits: -$75,000
- Cash paid for rent and utilities: -$20,000

- Cash paid for ministry expenses: -$25,000

Net cash provided by operating activities: $40,000

Investing Activities

- Cash used to purchase property: -$50,000
- Cash used to purchase equipment: -$10,000
- Net cash used in investing activities: -$60,000

Financing Activities

- Cash received from short-term loans: $20,000
- Cash received from long-term loans: $30,000
- Cash used to repay loans: -$10,000
- Net cash provided by financing activities: $40,000

Net increase in cash: $20,000

In this example, the church had a net increase in cash of $20,000 during the period covered by the cash flow statement. The church generated cash through tithes, offerings, and other donations, and used cash to pay for salaries, rent, utilities, and ministry expenses. The church also invested in property and equipment and received cash from short-term and long-term loans.

By reviewing the cash flow statement, the leaders of the church can gain a better understanding of how cash is flowing into and out of the organization. This can help them make informed decisions about budgeting, fundraising, and investing in the church's facilities and programs.

- **Budget vs actuals**

Comparing your actual financial performance to your budgeted financial performance can help you identify areas where you may need to adjust your spending or revenue-generating strategies.

The report typically includes the following components:

Budgeted income. This is the amount of income the organization expected to receive during the period covered by the report.

Actual income. This is the amount of income the organization actually received during the period covered by the report.

Budgeted expenses. This is the amount of money the organization budgeted to spend on various expenses during the period covered by the report.

Actual expenses. This is the amount of money the organization actually spent on various expenses during the period covered by the report.

Variance. This is the difference between the budgeted and actual income or expenses, expressed as a dollar amount and as a percentage.

Here is an example of a budget vs actual report for a hypothetical nonprofit organization:

Budgeted Income: $500,000
Actual Income: $450,000
Variance: -$50,000 (-10%)
Budgeted Expenses: $450,000
Actual Expenses: $475,000
Variance: +$25,000 (+5.5%)

In this example, the organization's actual income was lower than budgeted, resulting in a negative variance of $50,000 or 10 percent. The organization's actual expenses were higher than budgeted, resulting in a positive variance of $25,000 or 5.5 percent.

By reviewing the budget versus the actual report, leaders of churches, nonprofits, and Christian businesses can better understand how well they are managing their finances and where they need to make adjustments. For example, if actual expenses are consistently higher than budgeted expenses, the organization may need to find ways to reduce costs or adjust its budget. If actual income is consistently lower than budgeted income, the organization may need to focus on fundraising or other strategies to increase revenue.

- **Key performance indicators (KPIs)**

These are quantifiable measures of your organization's performance. They may include metrics such as revenue growth, profit margin, customer retention rate, or employee turnover rate. By tracking KPIs, you can assess your organization's progress toward achieving its goals.

The report typically includes a set of KPIs that are chosen based on the organization's goals and objectives. These KPIs can vary depending on the nature of the organization, but they should be quantifiable and measurable over time.

Here are some examples of KPIs that a church, nonprofit, or business might use:

Number of volunteers. This KPI measures the number of volunteers who are involved in the organization's programs and activities. It can help the organization track its capacity to serve its constituents and identify areas where more volunteers are needed.

Donation revenue. This KPI measures the amount of money the organization receives in donations. It can help the organization track its fundraising efforts and identify areas where it may need to increase its outreach.

Program attendance. This KPI measures the number of people who attend the organization's programs and events. It can help the organization track its impact and identify areas where it may need to improve its outreach and marketing.

Social media engagement. This KPI measures the number of likes, shares, and comments the organization receives on its social media channels. It can help the organization track its reach and engagement with its audience and identify areas where it may need to improve its messaging or social media strategy.

Customer acquisition cost (CAC). This KPI measures the cost of acquiring a new customer, helping a small business assess the effectiveness of its marketing and sales efforts.

Gross profit margin (GPM). This KPI measures the percentage of revenue remaining after deducting the cost of goods sold, allowing a small business to identify areas for improving profitability.

The KPI report typically includes data for each KPI over a period of time, such as a month or a quarter. The report may also include a comparison of the data with previous periods or benchmarks set by the organization.

It is important to note that every organization has two or three KPIs critical to its success and that affect the bottom line. These KPIs differ from organization to organization and depend on their goals and objectives. By reviewing the KPI report, leaders of churches, nonprofits, and Christian businesses can better understand how well they are achieving their goals and where they need to focus their efforts. They can use the data to make informed decisions about resource allocation, program development, and strategic planning.

Practice #5: Prepare for the Unexpected by Managing Risk and Establishing Emergency Funds

Financial stewardship involves more than just managing finances on a day-to-day basis. It also means being prepared for unexpected emergencies and crises.

In 2020, COVID-19 shook the world to its core. As the virus spread rapidly, the shockwaves reverberated throughout the globe, leaving businesses and individuals grappling with uncertainty and fear. My (Mac) company, Multiply Group, a consulting firm, was hit particularly hard. Much of our revenue was dependent on travel, and when air travel shut down, our income took a significant hit.

I still remember the sinking feeling in my gut as I watched our income drop over the next few months. It was a scary time. I had to consider the unthinkable: shutting down the company and finding employment elsewhere. It felt like all our hard work was for nothing.

Fortunately, when I was a young man, my father gave me the wise advice to always have an emergency fund. So, from the beginning of Multiply Group, we prioritized building up a reserve in our bank account that would protect us in times of financial difficulty.

Little did we know just how important that reserve would be. Only six months into starting our company, we faced a global pandemic that would drastically affect our income. But because we had that reserve, we were able to weather the storm and keep our company going.

Still, after nine months of relying on our reserves, we knew we needed a miracle to keep going. And so we prayed. We prayed for a specific amount that would replenish our reserves and keep our company operating. It was a desperate plea for help, and we had no idea what the future would hold.

That's when my friend Tim Wheat stepped in. When I asked him to pray with us for this amount, he challenged us to believe for double what we were praying for. At first, I was skeptical. But then I realized that sometimes, in desperate times, you need to borrow the faith of a friend.

And over the next ninety days, we saw God open doors, and clients started reaching out. It was nothing short of miraculous. Just as Tim had prayed, we received exactly double what we had originally prayed for. It was enough to replenish our reserves and enabled our ministry to continue.

Looking back on that time, I'm grateful for the lessons I learned. As a leader, it's important to be prepared for the unexpected. You never know when your organization may face a financial crisis, and it's up to you to keep your eyes on the financial health of your organization. Building up an emergency fund is just one way to manage unexpected risks. And sometimes, all it takes is a little faith and a lot of prayer to see you through the toughest of times.

So, as a CEO, nonprofit leader, or senior pastor, be proactive in managing risk and establishing an emergency fund of three to six months of reserves—act before a crisis hits. By preparing for the unexpected, you can ensure your organization's long-term financial health and stability.

Conclusion

Learning the skill of financial stewardship is not just a task; it's a transformative journey. It's about embracing obedience and dependence on God, grounding ourselves in biblical principles, aligning our financial plans with our organization's mission, regularly assessing our financial health, and fortifying our defenses against the unexpected.

This is not merely a set of practices; it's a commitment to shaping the future of your organization, ensuring its resilience, and ultimately, leaving a lasting kingdom impact.

Put It Into Practice

Developing a new skill requires practice. Before you meet with your trainer, complete the following assignments to help you practice financial stewardship.

(Note: Depending on the context and needs of the organization, these assignments may need to be adapted or modified.)

1. Create a Theology of Stewardship. Form a team, study relevant Scriptures, and collaborate to develop a unique Theology of Stewardship for your organization. Create a document that outlines your foundational biblical truths for financial stewardship and can be used for teaching and training purposes.

2. Conduct a personal financial self-assessment. Review your personal financial habits and practices in light of the biblical principles of financial stewardship. Write down your strengths and areas for improvement, and identify specific actions to steward your finances better.

3. Review and analyze your organization's financial statements. Gather your organization's financial statements (e.g., income statement, balance sheet, cash flow statement) and analyze them to assess your organization's financial health. Identify trends, opportunities, and areas for improvement, and use this information to inform your financial planning and decision-making.

4. Develop a comprehensive financial planning process. Use the guidelines provided in *Practice #3: Implement a Financial Planning Process that Supports Your Organization's Mission and Vision*. Collaborate with a team to create this document collectively, particularly if you are currently leading an organization.

5. Build a budget that aligns with your organization's mission and vision. Use your strategic financial plan to build a budgeting system that supports your organization's mission and vision. This budget should prioritize investments in areas that align with your organization's values and goals and should be flexible enough to adapt to changing circumstances.

6. Interview a leader from another organization about their financial planning process. Contact a leader of another organization and inquire about their financial planning process. Seek to gain insights from their accomplishments and difficulties and recognize techniques that could be adapted to your own organization. Where feasible, try to observe their budget planning process.

Reflect on Your Learning
Where did you grow the most in this competency?

What next step do you need to take to continue to grow in this competency?

Meet With Your Trainer

Consistent practice can be a great beginning to sharpening a skill, but developing a skill also requires processing what you learned with others.

Meet with your trainer and discuss what you learned from this module.

Dig Deeper

If you are leading or participating in an internship or want to continue to grow in the competency of financial stewardship, go to https://www.multiplygroup.org/internship-planner to download the companion guide to this book.

6

Leading Change

Navigating change as a leader can be like walking through a minefield, with risks and potential obstacles at every turn. Once, I (Mac) almost stepped on one of these landmines, but fortunately, my boss saved me in the nick of time. This metaphorical landmine could've blown up my opportunity to significantly impact the North American Mission Board's (NAMB) approach to church planting.

In 2015, I was hired by the NAMB to implement a church-planting system that I had developed a few years earlier. My task was to introduce this system to the thirty-two "Send Cities" across North America as efficiently as possible. I planned to do this by addressing the cities in a logical order. However, when I discussed the plan with my boss, he made significant changes to it. At first, I thought his plan seemed confusing and poorly thought out, but he explained that there were potential complications in certain cities that could make implementing the changes more difficult. He suggested we start with cities that were more open to the changes and build momentum before addressing those that may be more resistant. Ultimately, his approach proved successful, and even cities that initially resisted the changes eventually invited us to introduce the new assessment and training system.

Leading change is one of the most challenging and risky endeavors for a leader. It's not for the faint of heart, and many struggle to do it effectively. As someone who has navigated significant change in my organization, I know firsthand the potential consequences of ineffective leadership during change, such as:

- A loss of trust among your team
- Key leaders leaving the organization
- People feeling devalued
- Loss of momentum
- A more difficult time implementing future changes

The emotional responses triggered by change can make it even more difficult for leaders to navigate. That's why it's crucial to carefully consider the impact of change on your team and communicate the reasons, goals, and steps involved as clearly as possible. As a leader, it's essential to be patient and understanding when addressing questions and concerns from your team. Even though it may be challenging, you must make bold decisions and guide your team through successful change.

Few leaders have faced a more daunting change than the Old Testament character Joshua, who suddenly found himself leading the Hebrew people after Moses had led them for forty years. Moses had been more than just a leader; he had been their provider, protector, and guide through the wilderness. For Joshua, stepping into Moses' shoes was a daunting task, and it was not just the practicalities of leadership that made it difficult. The people who had followed Moses may have had doubts about Joshua's ability to lead them.

So, God reminded Joshua to be strong and courageous and not to be discouraged, assuring him that he would be with him wherever he went (Joshua 1:7–8).

This was not just empty rhetoric—God gave Joshua specific instructions to help him lead the people through the changes they were about to face. They would cross the Jordan River into the Promised Land, which was occupied by hostile nations that would need to be defeated. It was not going to be an easy task, but God promised Joshua he would be successful if he remained faithful and obedient to God's commands.

God empowered him to lead the people through the challenging changes ahead by reminding Joshua of the promise of success that came with his faithfulness and obedience. Joshua's task was not easy, but he could trust God's plan and guidance to bring them to victory.

The story of Joshua illustrates that change can be difficult for leaders to navigate, but it can be even more challenging for those around them. Change can have a personal impact on others, and the "why" behind the change may not always be clear to them. The key to successfully leading change is to have a clear vision and strategy, communicate it effectively, and provide support and encouragement to those affected by the change.

In this module, you will discover a six-point checklist for leading organizational change.

First, let's work to define our terms.

Character: *Composure*
Leaders consider and honor the perspectives of others, not taking disagreement personally.

Competency: *Leading Change*
Identify the meaningful change that needs to occur in the organization and communicate the changes in a way that honors those involved and brings the majority to embrace the change.

Objectives

1. Identify strategies for maintaining composure and fostering a positive work environment, even in challenging situations.
2. Assess motives for leading organizational change and how those motives align with the needs and goals of the organization.
3. Develop strategies for engaging key influencers in the change process and effectively communicating the compelling reason for the change to a diverse group of stakeholders.
4. Demonstrate empathy and emotional intelligence in leading organizational change and effectively navigate and address any resistance or challenges.
5. Discover how to implement actions to secure quick wins that help maintain a positive attitude throughout the change process.

Deepen Your Character:
Composure

Maintaining your composure as a leader is essential to effectively guide and inspire your organization. This means considering and honoring the perspectives of others, even if you disagree with them. Disharmony and division happen within a team or organization when you allow yourself to become reactive or take disagreement personally.

In today's fast-paced and often stressful world, it can be challenging to stay composed. It is natural to feel frustrated or upset when faced with obstacles or differing viewpoints. However, as a leader, it's essential to set an example and remain level-headed, regardless of resistance. This means finding ways to manage your emotions and reactions rather than letting them control you.

One way to do this is by adopting a growth mindset. Rather than seeing disagreement as a personal attack or a roadblock, try to view it as an opportunity to learn and grow. Seek out the perspectives of others, even if you don't initially agree with them (Proverbs 15:22; 27:17). This can help you gain a more holistic understanding of a situation and develop creative solutions that consider the needs and concerns of everyone involved.

As a pastor, I (Rick) knew that leading change in a church could be a difficult and emotional process. But I didn't fully understand the importance of maintaining composure until I faced a challenging situation with a member of our congregation named Sue.

Sue was from a more traditional church background, and she wasn't happy with the direction our church was headed. I kept hearing rumors she was complaining about me and critical of our new direction, but she never approached me directly. Eventually, she convinced her small group that I was wrong and she was right. Her husband invited our head elder and me to their group to discuss the direction of the church.

Even though I went into that meeting with our lead elder by my side, I still felt nervous and unsure of how the night would unfold. Sue and her small group confronted me with questions and accusations—attacking my character and motivations. It was a tough night, but as the meeting drew to a close, I knew we had done our best to honor Sue and her group, even in the face of their criticism.

A few weeks later, I learned that Sue and her family had found another church in town that better fit their values. And to my surprise, I received glowing feedback from members of Sue's small group. They had been impressed by our church leadership's willingness to answer their questions and appreciated our patience and understanding in the face of their concerns. Rather than turning against me, they had become even more enthusiastic about our church's direction.

Looking back on that experience, I realized that maintaining composure is crucial when leading change. We increase our credibility as leaders when we remain calm and collected in the face of conflict or resistance. We show that we are not defensive, and we are willing to listen to others' perspectives, even if we ultimately disagree.

But more than that, maintaining composure can also deepen our sense of conviction about the changes we are leading. When we face opposition, we have to dig deep and ask ourselves if we believe what we are doing is truly from God. That night, the experience with Sue and her small group strengthened my conviction that the changes were indeed God's will for our church.

So if you find yourself in a challenging leadership situation, remember the importance of maintaining composure. It's not always easy, but it can be a powerful tool for building credibility and strengthening your conviction. And who knows–you might even learn something new about yourself and your leadership in the process.

Scripture

As you read the following Scripture, meditate on what the author wishes to communicate, and answer the questions below. Allow the Holy Spirit to speak to you and challenge you as a leader about how you can develop your character so that you can maintain composure in your everyday life.

James 3:16-18

> For where you have envy and selfish ambition, there you find disorder and every evil practice. But the wisdom that comes from heaven is first of all pure; then peace-loving, considerate, submissive, full of mercy and good fruit, impartial and sincere. Peacemakers who sow in peace reap a harvest of righteousness.

In what situations do you struggle to maintain your composure as a leader? What triggers these reactions, and how can you better manage them in the future?

How can you apply the qualities described in James 3:16–18 (pure, peace-loving, considerate, submissive, full of mercy and good fruit, impartial and sincere) to your leadership style? What steps can you take to cultivate these qualities within yourself and model them for your team or organization?

How do you currently approach disagreement or conflicting viewpoints within your team or organization? What strategies can you employ to better consider and honor the perspectives of others?

How can you adopt a growth mindset when faced with challenges or disagreements as a leader? How can this mindset help you find creative solutions and foster a positive work environment?

Now that we have examined the character trait of composure, we can begin to work through the core competency for this module: *leading change*. As you read what follows, note how composure can undergird a leader's competency of leading change.

Develop Your Competency: *Leading Change*
Preassessment

Before proceeding, complete the assessment below. In the final module of this training guide, you will retake it as a postassessment to measure your transformation and growth in this competency.

The following proficiencies demonstrate mastery of this module's competency. For each of them, give yourself a grade of A, B, C, D, or E to reflect your actual level of competency today. Giving yourself an A+ indicates you are a model for others to follow. An E indicates that you feel you have no mastery.

Proficiency	Preassessment
I seek God fervently as I consider changes that need to be made to increase the organization's mission impact.	
I identify the pros and cons of the change and evaluate how individuals and groups will be affected by it.	
I involve key leaders in the change-planning process and seek buy-in before announcing or implementing changes.	

Proficiency	Preassessment
I design a communication plan to help people understand and accept the change.	
I model patience, self-control, and courage amid change, and guard against personal issues or selfish ambitions that could undermine progress.	

Which of the five proficiencies do you want to grow in the most? Why is it important for you to grow in that aspect?

What did you learn about your strengths and areas for improvement as a leader of change based on your assessment results?

> What specific actions do you plan to take to address any areas for improvement identified in the assessment?

A Checklist for Leading Change

My jaw dropped as I (Mac) read the first line of an article by Forbes, "Most companies that launch major change initiatives never make it to their stated ambition."[1]

Bain and Company's research shows that only 12 percent of change efforts succeed.[2] It's kind of scary when you think about it, especially for leaders who are always looking for ways to do things better and faster. But it's also a reminder of how important it is to learn to manage change effectively.

As leaders, we often have a unique perspective that allows us to see further and faster than others. We're always thinking about improving and serving our customers or constituents well. We're passionate about our mission and might even dream about it at night! It's unsurprising that we might think about a change for weeks or months before anyone else even hears about it. But we might face resistance when we announce the change too quickly and without giving context. The key is getting everyone on board with the change, especially those responsible for implementing it.

In this module, we will explore the challenges of leading change and provide a six-point checklist to help you navigate the process. We'll examine the importance of building buy-in, communicating effectively, and managing resistance and other key factors that can make or break a change initiative. By the end of this session, you'll have the tools you need to successfully lead change in your organization and achieve your stated ambition.

Checklist Item #1: Check Your Motives

Before embarking on any change initiative, it's important to take a moment to reflect on the motives driving the change. When our motives are pure, we can better serve those around us and avoid causing harm. However, if our motives are impure, it can create resistance to the change and harm those involved.

So, what are some impure motives for making changes? Here are a few to consider:

- Seeking approval from others
- Trying to validate our own self-worth
- Acting out of pride or a desire to be better than others
- Fear of losing people or influence
- Following a trend without considering its value or impact

As leaders, we must ask ourselves whether we seek to please God or people, whether we are leading with faith or fear, and whether we are following God's leading or just mimicking someone else's practices.

When our motives are pure, it will be evident to those around us, and they will be more likely to support the change. On the other hand, if our motives are impure, people may resist the change, and we may lose their trust.

It's essential to genuinely love and serve others rather than using them for our own gain. Only when our identity is rooted in Christ can we lead with pure motives that please God and benefit those we serve.

In the words of Timothy Keller, "Don't let success go to your head, nor let failure go to your heart."[3] That's why it's so important to examine our motives and ensure we are always leading with pure intentions.

> Think of some additional examples of impure motives for initiating change, and consider how you can recognize when you might be motivated by these factors.

Checklist Item #2: Engage Your Key Influencers

I used to get frustrated when I tried to lead change and encountered resistance. But then, a friend introduced me to the Diffusion of Innovations theory, which explains how an idea or product gradually spreads and becomes more popular over time. Communication theorist E. M. Rogers first introduced the theory in 1962, and it shows how different types of people respond to change and new ideas.

Rogers gives five categories of adopters.

Diffusion of Innovations Curve

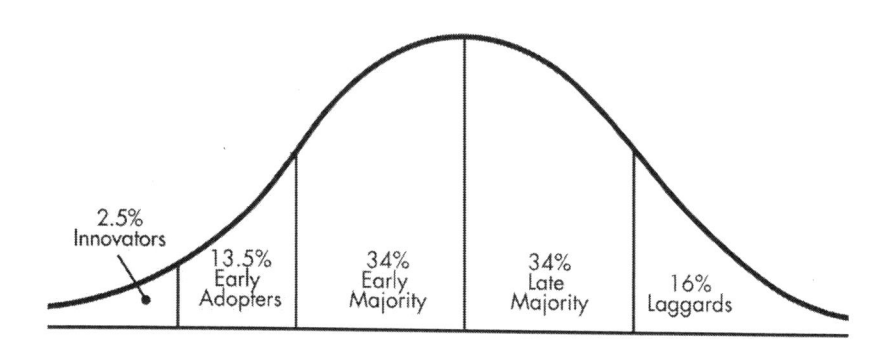

- 2.5% Innovators
- 13.5% Early Adopters
- 34% Early Majority
- 34% Late Majority
- 16% Laggards

- **Innovators**

The first 2.5 percent of people who adopt are called innovators. These people originate or are the first to try the innovation. They are interested in new ideas, comfortable with risk, and quickly adapt to change.

- **Early Adopters**

This group makes up the next 13.5 percent. They are aware of the need for change, are comfortable adapting to the change, and become essential voices in helping others understand the importance of the change. They don't need to be convinced; they just need the information to help them do their part to enact the change.

- **Early Majority**

Making up 34 percent, these people adopt new ideas before the average person; however, they wait until they see evidence that the change is working or beneficial.

- **Late Majority**

The next 34 percent are more resistant to embracing change. They are skeptical and won't adopt it until they see the early majority have bought in and feel the idea has been proven.

- **Laggards**

The final 13 percent of people are very conservative and the most difficult to convince of the necessity for change.

As you can see from the Diffusion of Innovations curve, leading change requires getting a lot of people bought into the change. And it also shows us that people relate to change in a variety of ways.

My (Mac) company, Multiply Group (www.multiplygroup.org), offers leadership pipeline training to churches. It's a year-long process where we help churches design a strategy for discipling leaders. We've noticed that staff members can resist the changes that come with this process, even if they agree that an intentional development strategy is needed. That's why we have the church create a leadership pipeline design team at the start of the training.

This team comprises key influencers who can help others understand and embrace the changes. It's important to involve these influencers because they are the early adopters and early majority and therefore, help others adapt to the changes that need to be made in order to create a culture of leadership development.

Leading change successfully requires recognizing that not everyone embraces change at the same pace. By understanding the Diffusion of Innovation theory and involving key influencers, you can create a more effective and sustainable change-management strategy. When key influencers are on board and actively supporting the change, it becomes easier to garner support from the entire team, ensuring a smoother and more successful transition. Remember, leadership is not just about implementing change from the top down;

it is about collaborating with those on the front lines to bring about positive and lasting transformation.

> What strategies could you use to engage key influencers in the change process and get their support for a new idea or product?

Checklist Item #3: Communicate a Compelling Why

Once you have checked your motives for making change and engaged your key influencers in the change, it's time to communicate the change to the larger audience.

A few years ago, I (Rick) stood on the platform of a five hundred-seat auditorium we needed to expand. We planned to open up an alcove and add balconies to create an additional three hundred seats. And to do that, we needed to raise $3 million.

I wanted our people to see the *why* behind the *what*. So I pointed to the back corner of where the balcony would be and said, "Three years from now, I can see a young woman in her late teens slipping into the church and sitting as far away from the front as possible. She's just found out she's pregnant. But here she is in our new balcony. She hears a message of hope. She finds an accepting community. She trusts Christ. She keeps her baby. She meets a young man. They marry. And together, they join me on this platform to dedicate that little life that was saved to Christ. We seek to expand our facility for people—for lives and families that will be changed forever."

One of the essential elements of successful change is people who share a vision of the future. Great leaders paint a compelling picture of the future, why it is essential, and how it will positively impact the kingdom.

Change requires sacrifice. People are not against sacrifice as long as they understand why they are making the sacrifice. Is there a compelling reason for the change you want to make? In his book *Leading Change*, leadership professor John Kotter refers to this as creating a sense of urgency.[4]

To communicate a compelling sense of urgency, we must address the *heads*, the *hearts*, and the *hands* of those we lead. In Romans 6:17, Paul thanks God for the change that had taken place in the lives of the Roman believers who had come to be "obedient [*hands*] from the *heart* to the standard of teaching [*head*] to which [they] were committed" (ESV, emphasis ours). People won't follow us into lasting change unless we appeal to the mind, the emotions, and the will.

- **Head**

The proposed change has to make sense biblically and rationally. It has to be defendable. You'll have to demonstrate how the change will please God and how it will serve people. This is your opportunity to stretch the minds of your people—encouraging them to believe in the God who can do abundantly beyond all that they can ask or imagine.

- **Heart**

You must engage the hearts of your people. What brings a tear to their eyes? What makes them pound the table and say, "This has to change"? Tell stories of changed lives. Create scenarios describing the kind of future your people will want to live in. Create a longing where the heart cry of your people is "If only this could happen..." Help your people care.

- **Hands**

Give them clear action steps. Help your people say, "We have to act, and we have to act now!" What will cause people to want to flex their muscles to help? Encourage your team to consider the advancements that could be made if everyone rolled up their sleeves and worked together. You want people to ask, "What must we do?"

> What are some ideas for effectively communicating the *why* behind a change?

How can you appeal to the head, heart, and hands in communicating about the change?

Checklist Item #4: Demonstrate Empathy

Once you communicate the change more broadly, you will begin hearing from those in the late majority or laggard category with less than positive emotions. So the next checklist item for change is demonstrating empathy for those who struggle with the change.

When I (Rick) led our church through a senior leadership transition, several long-time church members struggled with the change. I was the founding pastor who had led the church for twenty-six years. When we communicated an elder-approved, two-year transition plan to pass the torch to a new, younger lead pastor, some members were not on board.

One couple told me they intended to leave the church once the new lead pastor was inaugurated. The prospect of losing that family was difficult for me. I had performed their wedding ceremony and the wedding ceremonies of their sons, been on disaster relief mission trips with the husband, and performed the funeral services for the wife's parents. The relational equity I had with this couple (and they had with me) was significant.

Because of their influence in our faith community, I knew other families would likely follow them out. So, I invited them to a breakfast meeting at a local Panera Bread. I led with questions: "What are your primary concerns?" and "What questions do you have?" I tried to listen carefully and non-defensively. I tried to feel what they were feeling. I said things like, "I might feel that way, too."

After an hour of listening and learning, I asked, "Would you consider doing me a favor? Would you stay at CVC for at least one year and then reevaluate?" They did. And they grew to love our new lead pastor. I am so glad they stayed. Their influence in our missions and prayer ministries grew dramatically.

I don't always empathize well. But I am so glad that on this occasion, I slowed down enough to be a leader who listens first and empathized with a couple who struggled with the changes we were making.

People don't trust what they don't understand, and that can cause them to be resistant. Business psychologist Dr. Rachel Cotter Davis notes that there are typically four stages of change resistance: denial, anger, exploring, and acceptance.[5] I would add that at the end of this process, people may either reject or accept the change.

The leader's job is to recognize that change is not a one-size-fits-all process and that individuals may progress through the stages of change resistance at different paces. Leading with empathy involves understanding that each person's journey is unique and requires personalized support. As hard as it may be, we have to resist the temptation to dismiss resistance or push people to accept the change. Instead, we should continue to be patient and compassionate, providing the necessary space and resources for our team members to navigate their feelings and concerns.

Empathetic leadership also means acknowledging the emotional investment that team members may have in the organization. By expressing genuine appreciation for the contributions and history of those who are struggling with the change, we validate their experiences and demonstrate that their feelings matter. This approach fosters a sense of safety, encouraging open dialogue and honest expression of concerns.

Empathy extends beyond just listening; it includes taking proactive steps to address the root causes of resistance. Leaders should strive to communicate the *why* behind the change more effectively, helping team members grasp the purpose of the change. Transparent communication that addresses fears and uncertainties can alleviate resistance and build trust in the change process.

As you demonstrate empathy, you set an example for the entire organization, promoting a culture of understanding and compassion. By showing genuine care and concern for your team, you create an environment where individuals feel valued, heard, and supported. In turn, this fosters a more positive and receptive atmosphere for embracing change and achieving shared goals.

Empathy is not a sign of weakness but a powerful tool that fosters trust, strengthens relationships, and enables teams to navigate through change together successfully.

When facing resistance to change, are you more prone to enter "persuasion" or "empathizing" mode?

Think about two or three individuals resisting the change you are leading. What stage would you say they are in?

- Denial
- Anger
- Exploring
- Acceptance/Rejection

What is the next step you need to take with these individuals?

Checklist Item #5: Secure Quick Wins

Quick wins are a powerful tool for sparking lasting change. They are small, immediate successes that can help to build momentum and overcome resistance to change. By demonstrating the benefits of a new approach or idea, quick wins can help to establish credibility and create a sense of momentum that can inspire and motivate others to join.

For example, in sports, a single play or action can sometimes have a big impact on the outcome of a game. In football, one first down can lead to a series of first downs and, ultimately, a game-winning drive. In baseball, a walk or single hit can disrupt the opposing pitcher and give your team an advantage. And in basketball, a lay-up or three-pointer can spark a run of unanswered points. Similarly, small wins can add up to big changes over time in life and leadership.

Biblical leaders like David, Ezra, and Nehemiah also understood the power of quick wins. David secured a quick win by pronouncing a public blessing over the men who honorably buried his predecessor, King Saul (2 Samuel 2:5-6). Ezra began his mission to restore righteousness and worship in Jerusalem by leading the people of God in fasting and prayer (Ezra 8:21). And Nehemiah started the Jerusalem wall-building project with an initial victory, empowering Eliashib and his fellow priests to rebuild just one gate—the Sheep Gate (Nehemiah 3:1).

As a leader, it's important to spend time with God and ensure that your quick wins are not just good ideas but God's ideas. Quick wins can do more than just provide short-term benefits; they can also help to establish your credibility as a leader, give people something positive to focus on, create a sense of momentum, build a foundation for future change, and demonstrate that you are walking with God. So don't be afraid to pursue quick wins and use them to bring about lasting change.

How can quick wins help establish credibility and build momentum as a leader?

How can you ensure your quick wins align with God's will and purpose?

Checklist Item #6: Help Maintain a Healthy Attitude

As we have seen in this module, being a leader sometimes means leading change, which can be tough. It takes patience, perseverance, and a positive attitude to see the process through to the end. However, change is necessary for growth and progress.

As a leader, it's your job to help your team maintain a positive attitude throughout the change process, even though change can be scary and unsettling for some people. Below are some tips for doing so.

- **Communicate clearly and often**

Communication is crucial during times of change. Make sure to communicate the vision and goals of the change, as well as the steps involved in the process. Be transparent about the challenges and obstacles you may face along the way and invite feedback and suggestions from your team. Regular check-ins and progress reports help keep everyone on the same page and make them feel involved in the process.

- **Recognize and celebrate successes**

Change can be overwhelming, but it's important to celebrate the small victories along the way. This helps build momentum and keeps everyone motivated and engaged. Be sure to recognize and reward team members for their contributions and achievements throughout the process. Celebrating milestones can also help break the journey into smaller, more manageable steps.

- **Foster a positive culture**

A positive and supportive team culture is essential during times of change. Encourage open and honest communication, and make sure to actively listen to your team's concerns and feedback. Promote a growth mindset, where mistakes are seen as learning opportunities, and challenges are viewed as opportunities for growth. Lead by example and demonstrate a positive and resilient attitude despite setbacks or obstacles.

- **Provide support and resources**

Change can be challenging, and it's important to provide your team with the resources and support they need to succeed. This can include training, coaching, mentoring, and access to tools and technologies that can help streamline the change process. Encourage your team to take breaks and prioritize self-care, as this can help prevent burnout and keep everyone energized and focused.

> Consider a time when you experienced a major change in your organization. How did your leader handle it? Were they able to maintain a positive attitude, and if so, how did they help the team stay motivated and engaged?

What could they have done better?

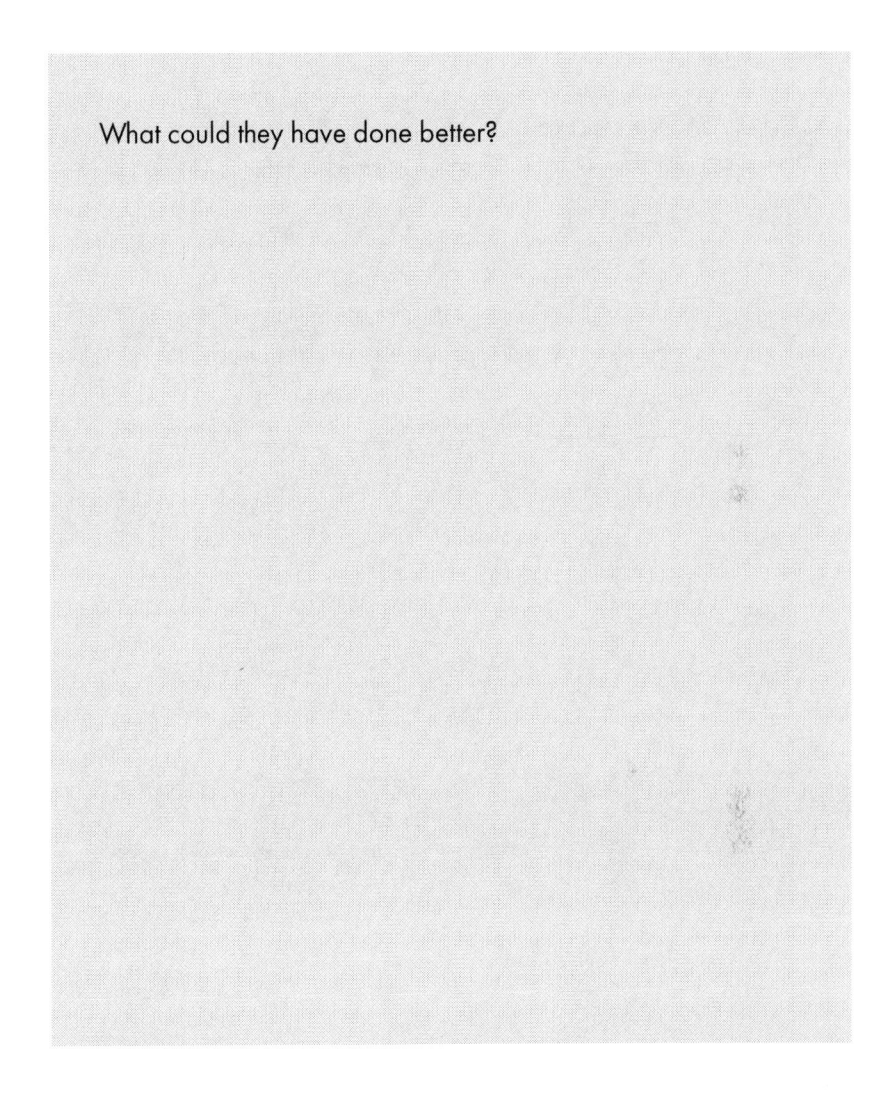

Conclusion

Remember, leading change isn't easy, but you can help your team navigate the process smoothly and effectively with the right attitude and approach. You can help your team maintain a healthy attitude and achieve success by communicating clearly, recognizing and celebrating successes, fostering a positive team culture, and providing support and resources.

Put It Into Practice

Developing a new skill requires practice. Before you get together with your trainer, complete a few of the following assignments to help you practice leading change.

1. Identify an area in your organization that needs change. Create a plan with specific steps, timelines, and resources. Seek feedback from your trainer before implementing.

2. Interview someone with experience in leading change. Prepare questions, take notes, and summarize your findings. Share these findings with your trainer.

3. Practice presenting your change plan to influential leaders. Practice with your trainer first. Focus on building rapport, explaining your rationale, and addressing concerns.

4. Hold a team meeting to discuss effective strategies for implementing change. Prepare an agenda, encourage everyone to share ideas and concerns, and document the outcomes.

5. Ask a team member to assess your leadership skills in leading change using the leading change proficiencies at the beginning of this module.

6. Research online the best practices for leading change. Summarize your findings and reflect on how you can apply them.

7. Lead your team in a book study on *Leading Change* by John Kotter. Schedule regular meetings to discuss and apply the concepts in the book.

Reflect on Your Learning

Where did you grow the most in this competency?

What next step do you need to take to continue to grow in this competency?

Meet With Your Trainer

Consistent practice can be a great beginning to sharpening a skill, but developing a skill also requires processing what you learned with others.

Meet with your trainer and discuss what you learned from this module.

Dig Deeper

If you are leading or participating in an internship or want to continue to grow in the competency of leading change, go to https://www.multiplygroup.org/internship-planner to download the companion guide to this book.

---

[1] David Michels, "Change Is Painful, And That's OK," *Forbes*, February 26, 2019, https://www.forbes.com/sites/davidmichels/2019/02/26/change-is-painful-and-thats-ok.

[2] Ibid.

[3] Timothy Keller (@timkellernyc), "Don't let success go to your head, nor let failure go to your heart," Twitter post, February 18, 2015, https://twitter.com/timkellernyc/status/568198307522224129.

[4] John P. Kotter, *Leading Change* (Brighton, MA: Harvard Business Review Press, 2012), 37.

[5] "What Neuroscience Teaches Us About Change Management," *Laserfiche*, https://www.laserfiche.com/resources/blog/what-neuroscience-teaches-us-about-change-management/.

[6] Kotter, *Leading Change*.

7

Review Your Progress

Congratulations! Over the past few weeks and months, you have worked your way through six leadership modules, met with your trainer to debrief and discover new insights, and grown in your leadership character and competencies.

During this training, you have had a trainer walk alongside you serving as a model, providing feedback on your leadership, and giving you insights to grow in your character and competency. While it may feel like this journey is over, it is really just beginning.

Leadership is a lifelong learning process. And a big part of that process is doing periodic self-evaluation to discover your strengths as well as the areas in which you need to continue to grow.

In this training guide, each module started by having you self-assess an aspect of your character. In each module you also did a self-assessment, scoring yourself A–E on five proficiencies of each leadership competency. Altogether you evaluated your leadership on thirty proficiencies!

The final step of this training is a postassessment. You can do this on your own or with your trainer. This is a tool that you can come back to again and again as you continue to grow in your ability to lead leaders.

Postassessment: *Character*

Now that you have interacted with the content, it is time to reflect on what you have learned. This is the step where you must ask yourself, "How do I need to continue to grow in this aspect of my *character*?" Answer the following character questions and share your reflections during your meeting time with your trainer.

Module 1: *Loyalty*

Leaders demonstrate a steadfast dedication to their cause, team, and values, even in the face of adversity.

What was the biggest thing you learned about this aspect of your character?

In what way have you seen growth in this area?

What next step do you need to take to continue growing in this aspect of your character?

Module 2: *Conviction*

Leaders consistently uphold and act in accordance with a set of core beliefs, regardless of external circumstances.

What was the biggest thing you learned about this aspect of your character?

In what way have you seen growth in this area?

What next step do you need to take to continue growing in this aspect of your character?

Module 3: *Submission*
Leaders listen to God's voice, know God's heart, and obediently follow God's will.

What was the biggest thing you learned about this aspect of your character?

In what way have you seen growth in this area?

What next step do you need to take to continue growing in this aspect of your character?

Module 4: *Confidence*
Leaders fully trust in the guidance of the Holy Spirit, enabling them to approach challenges and decisions with self-assurance and peace.

What was the biggest thing you learned about this aspect of your character?

In what way have you seen growth in this area?

What next step do you need to take to continue growing in this aspect of your character?

Module 5: *Generosity*

Leaders manage finances guided by biblical principles, enabling them to participate in God's work of transforming lives and communities.

What was the biggest thing you learned about this aspect of your character?

In what way have you seen growth in this area?

What next step do you need to take to continue growing in this aspect of your character?

Module 6: *Composure*
Leaders consider and honor the perspectives of others, not taking disagreement personally.

What was the biggest thing you learned about this aspect of your character?

In what way have you seen growth in this area?

What next step do you need to take to continue growing in this aspect of your character?

Postassessment: *Competency*

Now that you have interacted with the content and put it into practice, it is time to reflect on what you have learned. This is the step where you must ask yourself, "How do I need to continue to grow in this aspect of my *competency*?" Fill your preassessment results in the following tables and then score yourself again according to the degree of growth you feel you've experienced. (For example, you might have scored yourself a C in preassessment and a B in postassessment.) Giving yourself an A+ indicates you are a model for others to follow. An E indicates no mastery. Then answer the questions and share your reflections during your meeting time with your trainer.

Module 1: *Perseverance*

Unyielding dependence on God that fuels an unrelenting commitment to the mission in the face of difficulties, obstacles, or discouragements.

Where did you grow the most in this competency?

What next step do you need to take to continue to grow in this competency?

Proficiency	Preassessment	Postassessment	Notes
I intentionally cultivate my dependence on God and seek his guidance and strength as I face challenges and obstacles.			
I regularly study and reflect on God's Word—seeking wisdom and guidance to help me persevere through difficult situations.			
I prioritize my relationships with family, friends, and colleagues—recognizing that strong relationships provide support and encouragement when facing challenges.			

Proficiency	Preassessment	Postassessment	Notes
I consistently care for my physical and emotional health by eating well, exercising regularly, and getting enough sleep.			
I regularly assess my calling and purpose, seeking to align my goals and actions with God's plan for my life and make adjustments when necessary.			

Module 2: *Shaping Culture*

Proactively cultivate and embody the core values that drive a spiritually healthy and productive work environment.

Where did you grow the most in this competency?

What next step do you need to take to continue to grow in this competency?

Proficiency	Preassessment	Postassessment	Notes
I have a strong sense of conviction around each one of our organizational values.			
I prioritize open and ongoing communication with our team about our organizational values, regularly discussing how they inform our actions and decisions.			
I lead by example and intentionally model our organizational values in my own behavior, serving as a positive role model for others.			

Proficiency	Preassessment	Postassessment	Notes
I regularly evaluate the health and effectiveness of our organizational culture, working collaboratively with my team to identify areas of strength and areas for improvement.			
I use our organizational values to guide decisions, ensuring every action and choice aligns with our shared principles and priorities.			

Module 3: *Casting Vision*

Communicate a clear picture of the future in a way that motivates others to take actions that advance the God-given vision.

Where did you grow the most in this competency?

What next step do you need to take to continue to grow in this competency?

Proficiency	Preassessment	Postassessment	Notes
I prioritize prayer and dependence on God in capturing and communicating his vision for my organization or team.			
I articulate a clear and compelling vision that inspires others to take action.			
I identify and communicate opportunities and potential distractions in a way that aligns with the mission and values of my organization.			
I develop specific goals and objectives that help bring the vision to life.			

Proficiency	Preassessment	Postassessment	Notes
I regularly evaluate progress toward the vision and make necessary adjustments to keep the team on track.			

Module 4: *Teaching*
Impart knowledge, skills, and values to learners, inspiring and motivating them to actively engage in personal and spiritual growth.

Where did you grow the most in this competency?

What next step do you need to take to continue to grow in this competency?

Proficiency	Preassessment	Postassessment	Notes
I regularly apply the teachings I share to my own life and strive to be a living example of the message I deliver to others.			
I utilize various teaching techniques in my sermons and lessons to cater to people's short attention spans and make the message more engaging.			
I devote sufficient time to preparing and studying before delivering my teaching.			
I invest time researching and studying effective teaching methods to continually grow and improve as a teacher.			

Proficiency	Preassessment	Postassessment	Notes
I regularly evaluate my communication skills and seek feedback from others to improve my teaching abilities.			

Module 5: *Financial Stewardship*

Implement financial strategies that ensure financial sustainability while maintaining transparency, accountability, and compliance with legal and biblical standards.

Where did you grow the most in this competency?

What next step do you need to take to continue to grow in this competency?

Proficiency	Preassessment	Postassessment	Notes
I model biblical principles of financial stewardship in my personal and professional life.			
I seek to align our organization's financial practices with biblical stewardship principles, including generosity, integrity, and accountability.			
I understand our organization's financial goals, strategies, and metrics and how they support our mission and vision.			

Proficiency	Preassessment	Postassessment	Notes
I consistently analyze financial data, identify trends and opportunities, and use that information to inform strategic decisions and prioritize investments.			
I foster a culture of financial responsibility and accountability, promoting understanding and engagement with our financial goals and practices.			

Module 6: *Leading Change*
Identify the meaningful change that needs to occur in the organization and communicate the changes in a way that honors those involved and brings the majority to embrace the change.

Where did you grow the most in this competency?

What next step do you need to take to continue to grow in this competency?

Proficiency	Preassessment	Postassessment	Notes
I seek God fervently as I consider changes that need to be made to increase the organization's mission impact.			
I identify the pros and cons of the change and evaluate how individuals and groups will be affected by it.			
I involve key leaders in the change-planning process and seek buy-in before announcing or implementing changes.			
I design a communication plan to help people understand and accept the change.			

Proficiency	Preassessment	Postassessment	Notes
I model patience, self-control, and courage amid change, and guard against personal issues or selfish ambitions that could undermine progress.			

For the Trainer

As a leader yourself, you have much wisdom and insight to offer those who are in the process of becoming leaders too. The *Leading an Organization* training is designed to help these individuals gain the knowledge and experience they need to lead effectively.

As a trainer, you are both a model and a mentor. As a model, you allow those you are training to watch you demonstrate both the character and competency each module covers. You are the best curriculum others can read.

As a mentor, you observe and give trainees feedback as they put what they're learning into practice. Approach your time together in the spirit of a fellow learner rather than the spirit of an instructor. The mentoring component is accomplished better by training two to three people at one time rather than going through it one-on-one. When you have two or three, you'll have better discussions, and the participants will learn from one another as well.

Tips

Schedule
Before meeting with your trainees, create a proposed schedule of when and where you will meet. A biweekly rhythm should give them plenty of time to read the module and do the assignments. Remember, however, that the purpose is transformation—growth in the character and competency of those you are training—so do not rush modules.

Feel free to meet two or even three times for one module if you feel that's necessary. One of the beauties of this approach to training is you can have a flexible timeline.

Model

Modeling is one of the most effective means of training others. Invite the trainee to observe you in your leadership role so that you can model these particular competencies. For example, if you are casting vision in a meeting, teaching on the weekend, or doing a budget review with someone from your team, ask your trainees to come and observe. After they have observed you, ask them what they learned from watching you in action.

Meet

When you meet with those you are training, I recommend you schedule fifty to seventy-five minutes. Each module has more content than you can cover in that amount of time, so preview the questions and mark those that will bring out the most learning. Don't feel like you have to cover every single question, and feel free to ask follow-up questions to increase learning. But also don't jump back and forth within the module, because the content is arranged in an order that delivers maximum insight and practical learning. What follows is a general guide to a training meeting. Remember to be flexible and allow the Holy Spirit to use you to help each learner truly grasp and learn what God has for them in each module. A typical training session looks something like the following.

1. Connect (5–10 minutes)

Spend the first few minutes allowing the group to connect relationally and catch up on what's been going on in their week. Avoid just rushing into the content. Remember, this is a relational approach to development, which means allowing people time to get to know each other well.

2. Celebrate (5 minutes)

Ask, "What is something we've seen God do since the last time we met that we can celebrate?" You don't have to spend a lot of time on this, but take a few minutes and enjoy the work God is doing in your trainees' lives or ministries. This celebration time can reveal some important things in the lives of these leaders and can strengthen their faith as they watch how God is working in one another's lives.

3. Coach (30–45 minutes)

Walk through the questions and assessments. The trainee should have worked through all the content of the module before you meet with them, so you are asking them to discuss matters they have already considered and reflected on personally. The material provided is more than enough for a forty-five-minute discussion. Make sure you are prepared to discuss what is most relevant for your particular learners. (See "Facilitate" and "Assign" below.)

4. Communicate (1–2 minutes)

Ask, "What important upcoming events do we all need to be aware of?" You won't need to spend much more than one minute on this. But it is important to communicate any key events coming up at the church, as well as the details for your next training session.

5. Care (10–15 minutes)

Make sure you save time to ask, "How can we pray for each other?" Spend a few minutes praying with and for each other. While this is a general guide, remember to be flexible and allow the Holy Spirit to use you to help each learner truly grasp and learn what God has for them in each module.

Facilitate

Remember that as a trainer, you are a facilitator of discussion. It is important to get your trainees talking about what they learned. The temptation will be to talk too much and tell them everything you know about each of the topics. Although your experience and insights are important, it is just as important that your learners verbalize what they are learning. Utilize the questions to guide them to share what they are discovering, then share your insights as a supplement to their learning experience. In addition, I always tell my trainers, "The questions in the modules stimulate thought and provide good answers, but your follow-up questions are where your learners will find the gold." I recommend using the Five Hats to stimulate a deeper level of thinking. For example, let's say you asked, "What is your biggest struggle with casting vision?" And the trainee replied, "The vision is clear in my head, but when I start to share, it doesn't come out very clear. People seem motivated but unsure how they can jump in and contribute to the vision." Here are five options for how you might follow up on that answer.

1. Fisherman: Point of View Question

Ask for the person's perspective or point of view in order to discover opportunity or obstacles. From the example above I might ask, "Why do you think the vision is clear in your head but doesn't come out clear when you share it?"

2. Reporter: Story Question

Draw out a story from the person's past experience on the topic in order to discover a leadership insight. I might ask, "You said people seem motivated but don't jump in and contribute to the vision. Can you share an example of when this has happened? What did you learn from that experience?"

3. Physician: Self-Assessment Question

Ask the individual to diagnose themselves in order to discover their strengths or weaknesses. I might ask, "On a scale of 1–5, with 5 being high, how would you rate your ability to invite people into a next step of the vision you cast? Why did you choose [insert number they chose]? What do you need to do to grow to a [insert one number higher than they chose]?"

4. Contractor: List Building Question

Ask the individual or group to identify a list or framework to discover different perspectives or insights. I might ask, "What are four specific insights you gained from reading this module on vision that you can put into practice?"

5. Pilot: Action Step Question

After a member has highlighted something to work on, ask the individual to identify a flight path—practical next steps that will guide them in the direction of growth and development. I might ask, "What is the most important next step you need to take to enhance the clarity of your vision casting?"

Assign

While each module provides "Put It Into Practice" assignments, feel free to change those to give them assignments that fit the particular ministry role they are being trained for.

Module Questions

All the questions from the modules have been organized in a simple way on the following pages so you can seamlessly flow through the training questions to help those you are training learn from what they've read and put into practice.

Module 1: Perseverance

In this module, we will explore the competency of perseverance and its connection to the character trait of loyalty.

Deepen Your Character: *Loyalty*

Let's begin by focusing on the character portion of this study. In this module the focus is on **Loyalty**—*Leaders demonstrate a steadfast dedication to their cause, team, and values, even in the face of adversity.*

(Read Ruth 1:1–18 together.)

Ruth 1:1–18

In the days when the judges ruled, there was a famine in the land. So a man from Bethlehem in Judah, together with his wife and two sons, went to live for a while in the country of Moab. The man's name was Elimelek, his wife's name was Naomi, and the names of his two sons were Mahlon and Kilion. They were Ephrathites from Bethlehem, Judah. And they went to Moab and lived there. Now Elimelek, Naomi's husband, died, and she was left with her two sons. They married Moabite women, one named Orpah and the other Ruth. After they had lived there about ten years, both Mahlon and Kilion also died, and Naomi was left without her two sons and her husband. When Naomi heard in Moab that the Lord had come to the aid of his people by providing food for them, she and her daughters-in-law prepared to return home from there. With her two daughters-in-law she left the place where she had been living and set out on the road that would take them back to the land of Judah. Then Naomi said to her two daughters-in-law,

"Go back, each of you, to your mother's home. May the LORD show you kindness, as you have shown kindness to your dead husbands and to me. May the LORD grant that each of you will find rest in the home of another husband." Then she kissed them goodbye and they wept aloud and said to her, "We will go back with you to your people." But Naomi said, "Return home, my daughters. Why would you come with me? Am I going to have any more sons, who could become your husbands? Return home, my daughters; I am too old to have another husband. Even if I thought there was still hope for me—even if I had a husband tonight and then gave birth to sons—would you wait until they grew up? Would you remain unmarried for them? No, my daughters. It is more bitter for me than for you, because the LORD'S hand has turned against me!" At this they wept aloud again. Then Orpah kissed her mother-in-law goodbye, but Ruth clung to her. "Look," said Naomi, "your sister-in-law is going back to her people and her gods. Go back with her." But Ruth replied, "Don't urge me to leave you or to turn back from you. Where you go I will go, and where you stay I will stay. Your people will be my people and your God my God. Where you die I will die, and there I will be buried. May the LORD deal with me, be it ever so severely, if even death separates you and me." When Naomi realized that Ruth was determined to go with her, she stopped urging her.

- What do you imagine Ruth sacrificed to move to Judah with Naomi? In what way have you sacrificed recently for the sake of your team?
- What lessons can be learned from Ruth's story about the power of loyalty in building strong relationships and creating a sense of belonging within a team or community?

- In what practical ways can you cultivate loyalty in your team or organization?

Develop Your Competency: *Perseverance*

Now that we've talked about how we can grow in loyalty, let's talk through what you learned about the competency: **Perseverance**—*Unyielding dependence on God that fuels an unrelenting commitment to the mission in the face of difficulties, obstacles, or discouragements.*

How did you answer the following questions in the preassessment?

- Which of the five proficiencies do you want to grow in the most? Why is it important for you to grow in that aspect?
- Which of the five perseverance proficiencies do you feel strongest in, and why?
- Looking at your overall proficiency assessment, what areas must you focus on to become a more effective and resilient leader? What steps can you take to prioritize those areas and make meaningful progress?

Cultivate a Dependence on the Holy Spirit

- In what ways have you been tempted to rely on your own strength and abilities instead of depending on the Holy Spirit in your life and ministry?
- What must you do to intentionally cultivate a deeper relationship with God and abide in him to avoid burnout and failure?

Establish a Christ-Centered Identity

- Think of a leader you know who is secure in God's love. How did that leader grow to be so secure?

Prioritize Physical Health

- How would you assess the condition of your physical health? Unhealthy, Average Health, or Very Healthy?
- Which of the four areas is your strongest: Eat, Sleep, Move, or Think? Weakest?
- What next step do you need to take to improve your physical health?

Set Clear Boundaries

- Which of these boundary areas do you struggle with the most? What next steps do you need to take to strengthen that boundary? Who can you discuss this with to help you or hold you accountable?

Put It Into Practice

Developing a new skill requires practice. Discuss with those you are training what they learned about perseverance from their "Put It Into Practice" assignments.

1. Identify a problem in your area of leadership and assess your attitude toward the issue. Spend extended time in prayer regarding that challenge. Journal your thoughts and insights on the character of God and your own character during this season. Consider how you

can rely more fully on God's strength and wisdom as you persevere. Then brainstorm a list of solutions to overcome this challenge and commit to implementing one of the solutions. Meet with a mentor to discuss your progress and receive feedback on your perseverance.

2. Coach a leader whose morale seems low due to a challenge and help them develop a healthy perspective. This will require patience, empathy, and a willingness to invest time and energy in someone else's growth.

3. Search for Scripture passages about perseverance, and write them in a journal. Write a one-page journal entry, expressing what God impresses on your heart about this competency. Meditate on these verses regularly and ask God to give you the strength to persevere through difficulties.

4. Research how other leaders have persevered through difficult situations. Google "How successful Christian leaders persevere" and write a summary of what you learned. Use these insights to inform your own approach to perseverance.

5. Interview a leader with a long tenure in their role, and ask them what they have learned about perseverance. Journal your insights from the conversation and share them with your trainer.

Reflect on Your Learning

- Where did you grow the most in this competency?
- What next step do you need to take to continue to grow in this competency?

Module 2: Shaping Culture

In this module, we will focus on the character trait of conviction and key strategies that can help you shape your organization's culture and drive success.

Deepen Your Character: *Conviction*

Let's begin by focusing on the character portion of this study. In this module the focus is on **Conviction**— *Leaders consistently uphold and act in accordance with a set of core beliefs, regardless of external circumstances.*

(Read John 2:3–17 together.)

John 2:3–17

When it was almost time for the Jewish Passover, Jesus went up to Jerusalem. In the temple courts he found people selling cattle, sheep and doves, and others sitting at tables exchanging money. So he made a whip out of cords, and drove all from the temple courts, both sheep and cattle; he scattered the coins of the money changers and overturned their tables. To those who sold doves he said, "Get these out of here! Stop turning my Father's house into a market!" His disciples remembered that it is written: "Zeal for your house will consume me."

- If you were one of Jesus' followers at this time, what would be going through your mind as you watched Jesus take this stand in the temple?
- Jesus is still in his first year of public ministry at this point. What were some of the potential consequences you might

expect as a result of Jesus' actions? Why do you think it was important Jesus took this stand at the beginning of his public ministry?

- Think of a leader you know who demonstrates deep conviction. How is that conviction demonstrated in their leadership actions?
- Where do you demonstrate conviction? Where do you need to demonstrate greater levels of conviction?

Develop Your Competency: *Shaping Culture*

Now that we have examined the character trait of conviction, let's talk through what you learned about the competency: **Shaping Culture**—*Proactively cultivate and embody the core values that drive a spiritually healthy and productive work environment.*

How did you answer the following questions in the preassessment?

- Which of the five proficiencies do you want to grow in the most? Why is it important for you to grow in that aspect?
- Which of the values of your organization do you live out the best? The least? What steps do you need to take to live out the values more consistently?

Communication—Share the Values

- What can you do to increase the visibility of your organization's values?
- How are you currently using stories to shape the culture you

desire? What can you do to improve the way you use stories to shape the culture of your organization?
- What is one value you feel is important for you to model for your team right now? Why?

Expectation—Evaluate the Values

- How often do you and your team evaluate your organization's or group's values?
- What specific strategies do you use to ensure that the values are being lived out consistently?
- How can you ensure everyone is held accountable for adhering to the values and minimizing value drift?

Put It Into Practice

Developing a new skill requires practice. Discuss with those you are training what they learned about shaping culture from their "Put It Into Practice" assignments.

1. If you are considering starting a church, nonprofit, or business, take some time to write down four to six core values you want to see as part of the organization's culture. These values should be reflective of the kind of culture you want to establish and the goals you hope to achieve. Once you have identified these values, share them with a mentor, friend, or colleague, and get their feedback. Think about how you can make these values central to everything you do, from hiring and training employees to making key decisions.

2. Write down four to six core values you want to see as part of your family's culture. These values should be reflective of the kind of family

you want to have and the goals you hope to achieve as a family. Once you have identified these values, discuss them with your family and get their input. Consider how you can make these values a part of your daily life and use them to shape the way you interact with one another. Set aside regular family meetings to discuss how you are doing as a family in living out these values and to make any necessary adjustments.

3. Think of a person or organization whose culture you admire. Write down the values you believe are driving that culture. Then, think about ways that you can incorporate those values into your own life or organization. Consider how you can adapt those values to your unique situation, and consider how to make them central to everything you do.

4. Gather your team and evaluate how well you are living out the values of your organization's culture. Start by writing down your organization's values and giving it a letter grade of A, B, C, D, or E based on how well you believe you are living out that value. Do this individually and then come together to discuss your evaluations.

During the team discussion, identify any discrepancies or disagreements and work to reach a consensus on the grade for each value. Once you have agreed on the grades, work together to plan action steps to strengthen how you live out the values. Assign responsibilities for each action step and set deadlines for implementation.

Remember, the goal of this assignment is not to assign blame or criticize each other but rather to work together to identify areas where you can improve as a team and develop a plan to strengthen your culture.

Reflect on Your Learning

- Where did you grow the most in this competency?
- What next step do you need to take to continue to grow in this competency?

Module 3: Casting Vision

In this module, we will explore the practices necessary for leaders to successfully move their organization toward God's vision.

Deepen Your Character:
Submission

Let's begin by focusing on the character portion of this study. In this module the focus is on **Submission**—*Leaders listen to God's voice, know God's heart, and obediently follow God's will.*

(Read Acts 16:6–10 together.)

Acts 16:6–10

Paul and his companions traveled throughout the region of Phrygia and Galatia, having been kept by the Holy Spirit from preaching the word in the province of Asia. When they came to the border of Mysia, they tried to enter Bithynia, but the Spirit of Jesus would not allow them to. So they passed by Mysia and went down to Troas. During the night Paul had a vision of a man of Macedonia standing and begging him, "Come over to Macedonia and help us." After Paul had seen the vision, we got ready at once to leave for Macedonia, concluding that God had called us to preach the gospel to them.

- God prevented Paul's team from returning to Asia twice before revealing his plan for them to go to Macedonia. What emotions do you imagine Paul felt when he was prevented from moving forward with his plan? In what ways can you relate to Paul's situation?
- What do you think would have been the most difficult part for Paul in submitting to this change of plans?

- Which of the "submission saboteurs" do you struggle with the most (Comparison Trap, Distraction Trap, or People-Pleasing Trap), and how can you work to combat it?
- How can you create space in your life to intentionally listen for God's direction and guidance?
- In what specific areas of your leadership or vision do you need to intentionally create space to listen for God's direction and guidance?

Develop Your Competency: Casting Vision

Now that we have examined the character trait of submission, let's talk through what you learned about the competency: **Casting Vision**—*Communicate a clear picture of the future in a way that motivates others to take actions that advance the God-given vision.*

How did you answer the following questions in the preassessment?

- Which of the five proficiencies do you want to grow in the most? Why is it important for you to grow in that aspect?
- How has your ability to cast a clear and compelling vision improved over time?
- In what ways have you relied on your own strength and understanding rather than seeking God's guidance and direction in casting a vision for your organization?

What Is Our Mission?

- How does your organization's mission statement inform your day-to-day decisions and actions? Are there any areas where you feel it falls short or needs improvement?

- If you don't currently have a mission statement, try using our Mission Statement Tool. Share your draft with a mentor or colleague and get their feedback.

Where Have We Been (Rearview)?

- Now, take some time to fill out the Rearview: Where have we been? section of the Vision Scope tool.

What Opportunities Are Presenting Themselves That May Be Distractions and Could Get Us Off Course (Starboard View)?

- Use the Vision Scope tool to answer question #5 to identify opportunities that may be a distraction from your organization's vision.

What Are the Dangers We Need to Be Aware of as We Move Forward (Port View)?

- Use the Vision Scope tool to answer question #6 to identify potential dangers to your organization's vision.

Put It Into Practice

Developing a new skill requires practice. Discuss with those you are training what they learned about casting vision from their "Put It Into Practice" assignments.

1. Schedule a prayer retreat to seek God's vision for your organization or future venture. Spend time in solitude, seeking God's guidance

through prayer, and then meet with your trainer to share what God revealed to you.

2. Write a mission statement for your organization or revise your current one by focusing on four key elements—passion, strengths, problem, and Holy Spirit promptings. This statement should capture the heart of your organization and provide a clear direction for your team. After creating or revising your mission statement, share it with your trainer for feedback and guidance.

3. Develop an "elevator pitch" for your vision: craft a thirty-second pitch that communicates your vision clearly and concisely. This is a great exercise to practice communicating your vision to others and ensuring it is easily understandable and compelling. Share that elevator pitch with your trainer to get their feedback.

4. Working with your team, choose a one-year battle cry for your organization, which will serve as the main focus for the next twelve months. Write a summary statement that clearly and concisely states the big priority focus for the year. Next, identify four to five key objectives that will support the one-year battle cry and help achieve it. These objectives should be specific and measurable, with clear timelines and assigned responsibilities. Ensure everyone on your team understands how their department and role tie into achieving the one-year battle cry. Once you have identified the one-year battle cry and key objectives, share these with your trainer.

5. Hold a vision-casting meeting: schedule a meeting with your team to cast the vision and gain buy-in. Use the Vision Scope, the one-year battle cry, and the side-view questions to guide the meeting. This will

help everyone understand the vision, how it relates to their roles, and how they can contribute to its achievement.

Reflect on Your Learning

- Where did you grow the most in this competency?
- What next step do you need to take to continue to grow in this competency?

Module 4: Teaching

In this module, we will focus on the character trait of confidence and the competency of teaching.

Deepen Your Character: *Confidence*

Let's begin by focusing on the character portion of this study. In this module the focus is on **Confidence**—*Leaders fully trust in the guidance of the Holy Spirit, enabling them to approach challenges and decisions with self-assurance and peace.*

(Read Proverbs 3:5–6 together.)

Proverbs 3:5-6

Trust in the LORD with all your heart and lean not on your own understanding; in all your ways submit to him, and he will make your paths straight.

- What stands out to you the most from this passage?
- In what area of your teaching or preaching do you find it most challenging to trust in the Lord rather than relying on your own understanding?
- What steps can you take to cultivate God-confidence in your role as a teaching leader?

Develop Your Competency: *Teaching*

Now that we have examined the character trait of confidence, let's talk through what you learned about the competency: **Teaching**—*Impart knowledge, skills, and values to learners, inspiring* *and motivating them to actively engage in personal and spiritual growth.*

How did you answer the following questions in the preassessment?

- Which of the five proficiencies do you want to grow in the most? Why is it important for you to grow in that aspect?
- What did you learn about your teaching style and methods from taking this assessment?
- Were there any surprises or areas that you identified as needing improvement?
- What is the most important next step you need to take to grow as a teaching leader?

Live Out the Truth You Teach

- On a scale of 1–5, how often do you intentionally live out the truths you teach in your personal life and leadership?
- What obstacles or challenges do you encounter in integrating these truths into your life? What steps can you take to ensure you consistently model the truths you teach?

Prepare Your Mind

- Think of an experienced communicator you can speak with to learn about their preparation practices. What specific questions will you ask them to gain insights into their process?
- How can you better prioritize preparation time in your schedule to ensure you are adequately prepared for upcoming presentations or training?

- What are your thoughts and feelings about incorporating the practice of collecting illustrations into your weekly routine? What benefits do you think it could bring to your communication style?

Embrace Continuous Growth

- What is your greatest strength as a teacher? How could you grow that strength to the next level?

Regularly Evaluate Your Effectiveness

- Describe an approach to message evaluation you would enjoy and benefit from the most.

Put It Into Practice

Developing a new skill requires practice. Discuss with those you are training what they learned about teaching from their "Put It Into Practice" assignments.

1. Put together and deliver a ten-minute devotion or a full sermon using Andy Stanley's Me-We-God-You-Us outline. Ask your trainer and others to give feedback on what you did well and what you could do to grow as a communicator.

2. Observe a preacher/teacher you admire, and take note of the teaching style and delivery of the instructor. Share what you learn with your trainer.

3. Structure and deliver a training session using some of the techniques you learned in this module. Get feedback from your trainer.

4. Read a book on preaching or teaching and go through it with a friend or your trainer. Here are a few recommendations:

- Dr. Howard Hendricks, *Teaching to Change Lives: Seven Proven Ways to Make Your Teaching Come Alive*
- Timothy Keller, *Preaching: Communicating Faith in an Age of Skepticism*
- Haddon W. Robinson, *Biblical Preaching: The Development and Delivery of Expository Messages*
- Andy Stanley and Lane Jones, *Communicating for a Change: Seven Keys to Irresistible Communication*
- Bruce Wilkinson, *The Seven Laws of the Learner: How to Teach Almost Anything to Practically Anyone*

5. Interview a communicator and ask the following questions:

- Tell me about your preparation process.
- How do you engage your audience?
- How do you evaluate your own performance?
- What advice would you give to someone just starting out as a communicator?

Reflect on Your Learning

- Where did you grow the most in this competency?
- What next step do you need to take to continue to grow in this competency?

Module 5: Financial Stewardship

In this module, we will examine the character trait of generosity and the competency of financial stewardship and explore how these work together.

Deepen Your Character: *Generosity*

Let's begin by focusing on the character portion of this study. In this module the focus is on **Generosity**—*Leaders manage finances guided by biblical principles, enabling them to participate in God's work of transforming lives and communities.*

(Read 1 Chronicles 29:1–9 together.)

1 Chronicles 29:1–9

Then King David said to the whole assembly: "My son Solomon, the one whom God has chosen, is young and inexperienced. The task is great, because this palatial structure is not for man but for the LORD God. With all my resources I have provided for the temple of my God—gold for the gold work, silver for the silver, bronze for the bronze, iron for the iron and wood for the wood, as well as onyx for the settings, turquoise, stones of various colors, and all kinds of fine stone and marble—all of these in large quantities. Besides, in my devotion to the temple of my God I now give my personal treasures of gold and silver for the temple of my God, over and above everything I have provided for this holy temple: three thousand talents of gold (gold of Ophir) and seven thousand talents of refined silver, for the overlaying of the walls of the buildings, for the gold work and the silver work, and for all the work to be done by the craftsmen. Now, who is willing to consecrate themselves to the LORD today?" Then the leaders of families, the officers of the tribes of Israel, the commanders of thousands and commanders of hundreds, and the officials in charge of the king's work gave willingly. They gave toward the work on the temple of God five thousand talents and ten thousand darics of gold, ten thousand talents of silver, eighteen thousand talents of bronze and a hundred thousand talents of iron. Anyone who had precious stones gave them to the treasury of the temple of the LORD in the custody of Jehiel the Gershonite. The people rejoiced at the willing response of their leaders, for they had given freely and wholeheartedly to the LORD. David the king also rejoiced greatly.

- What do you learn from David about generosity in this passage?
- In what ways have you recently demonstrated generosity? How can you continue cultivating a spirit of generosity in your life and leadership?
- How can you encourage a culture of generosity and joy in giving among your team?

Develop Your Competency: *Financial Stewardship*

Now that we have examined the character trait of generosity, let's talk through what you learned about the competency: **Financial Stewardship**—*Implement financial strategies that ensure financial sustainability while maintaining transparency, accountability, and compliance with legal and biblical standards.*

How did you answer the following questions in the preassessment?

- Which of the five proficiencies do you want to grow in the most? Why is it important for you to grow in that aspect?
- Which of the five proficiency statements do you feel most confident in? Why?
- Which of the five proficiency statements do you feel least confident in? Why?
- What steps can you take to improve in the areas where you are least proficient?

Commit to Financial Obedience and Dependence on God

- Have you ever struggled with giving first to God and trusting him to provide? How can you apply the lessons from Rick and Maryanne's experience to your own life?
- Can you think of a time when a leader's generosity inspired you to give more?

Commit to a Foundation of Biblical Financial Stewardship

- If you were to write a Theology of Stewardship to help guide your organization, what two or three core beliefs would you want to include?

Implement a Financial Planning Process that Supports Your Organization's Mission and Vision

- What potential risks do you envision in an organization that doesn't have a detailed, written financial planning process they use each year?
- Have you or your organization ever used a vision-based

budgeting process? If so, how did it work for you? If not, would you consider implementing one? Why or why not?

Put It Into Practice

Developing a new skill requires practice. Discuss with those you are training what they learned about financial stewardship from their "Put It Into Practice" assignments.

1. Create a Theology of Stewardship. Form a team, study relevant Scriptures, and collaborate to develop a unique Theology of Stewardship for your organization. Create a document that outlines your foundational biblical truths for financial stewardship and can be used for teaching and training purposes.

2. Conduct a personal financial self-assessment. Review your personal financial habits and practices in light of the biblical principles of financial stewardship. Write down your strengths and areas for improvement, and identify specific actions to steward your finances better.

3. Review and analyze your organization's financial statements. Gather your organization's financial statements (e.g., income statement, balance sheet, cash flow statement) and analyze them to assess your organization's financial health. Identify trends, opportunities, and areas for improvement, and use this information to inform your financial planning and decision-making.

4. Develop a comprehensive financial planning process. Use the guidelines provided in *Practice #3: Implement a Financial Planning Process that Supports Your Organization's Mission and Vision.*

Collaborate with a team to create this document collectively, particularly if you are currently leading an organization.

5. Build a budget that aligns with your organization's mission and vision. Use your strategic financial plan to build a budgeting system that supports your organization's mission and vision. This budget should prioritize investments in areas that align with your organization's values and goals and should be flexible enough to adapt to changing circumstances.

6. Interview a leader from another organization about their financial planning process. Contact a leader of another organization and inquire about their financial planning process. Seek to gain insights from their accomplishments and difficulties and recognize techniques that could be adapted to your own organization. Where feasible, try to observe their budget planning process.

Reflect on Your Learning

- Where did you grow the most in this competency?
- What next step do you need to take to continue to grow in this competency?

Module 6: Leading Change

In this module, you will discover a six-point checklist for leading organizational change.

Deepen Your Character: *Composure*

Let's begin by focusing on the character portion of this study. In this module the focus is on **Composure**—*Leaders consider and honor the perspectives of others, not taking disagreement personally.*

(Read James 3:16–18 together.)

James 3:16–18

For where you have envy and selfish ambition, there you find disorder and every evil practice. But the wisdom that comes from heaven is first of all pure; then peace-loving, considerate, submissive, full of mercy and good fruit, impartial and sincere. Peacemakers who sow in peace reap a harvest of righteousness.

- In what situations do you struggle to maintain your composure as a leader? What triggers these reactions, and how can you better manage them in the future?
- How can you apply the qualities described in James 3:16–18 (pure, peace-loving, considerate, submissive, full of mercy and good fruit, impartial and sincere) to your leadership style? What steps can you take to cultivate these qualities within yourself and model them for your team or organization?
- How do you currently approach disagreement or conflicting viewpoints within your team or organization? What strategies

can you employ to better consider and honor the perspectives of others?
- How can you adopt a growth mindset when faced with challenges or disagreements as a leader? How can this mindset help you find creative solutions and foster a positive work environment?

Develop Your Competency: *Leading Change*

Now that we have examined the character trait of composure, let's talk through what you learned about the competency: **Leading Change**—*Identify the meaningful change that needs to occur in the organization and communicate the changes in a way that honors those involved and brings the majority to embrace the change.*

How did you answer the following questions in the preassessment?

- Which of the five proficiencies do you want to grow in the most? Why is it important for you to grow in that aspect?
- What did you learn about your strengths and areas for improvement as a leader of change based on your assessment results?
- What specific actions do you plan to take to address any areas for improvement identified in the assessment?

Check Your Motives

- Think of some additional examples of impure motives for initiating change, and consider how you can recognize when you might be motivated by these factors.

Engage Your Key Influencers

- What strategies could you use to engage key influencers in the change process and get their support for a new idea or product?

Communicate a Compelling Why

- What are some ideas for effectively communicating the *why* behind a change?
- How can you appeal to the head, heart, and hands in communicating about the change?

Demonstrate Empathy

- When facing resistance to change, are you more prone to enter "persuasion" or "empathizing" mode?
- Think about two or three individuals resisting the change you are leading. What stage would you say they are in?
    - Denial
    - Anger
    - Exploring
    - Acceptance/Rejection

What is the next step you need to take with these individuals?

Secure Quick Wins

- How can quick wins help establish credibility and build momentum as a leader?

- How can you ensure your quick wins align with God's will and purpose?

Help Maintain a Healthy Attitude

- Consider a time when you experienced a major change in your organization. How did your leader handle it? Were they able to maintain a positive attitude, and if so, how did they help the team stay motivated and engaged?
- What could they have done better?

Put It Into Practice

Developing a new skill requires practice. Discuss with those you are training what they learned about leading change from their "Put It Into Practice" assignments.

1. Identify an area in your organization that needs change. Create a plan with specific steps, timelines, and resources. Seek feedback from your trainer before implementing.

2. Interview someone with experience in leading change. Prepare questions, take notes, and summarize your findings. Share these findings with your trainer.

3. Practice presenting your change plan to influential leaders. Practice with your trainer first. Focus on building rapport, explaining your rationale, and addressing concerns.

4. Hold a team meeting to discuss effective strategies for implementing change. Prepare an agenda, encourage everyone to share ideas and concerns, and document the outcomes.

5. Ask a team member to assess your leadership skills in leading change using the leading change proficiencies at the beginning of this module.

6. Research online the best practices for leading change. Summarize your findings and reflect on how you can apply them.

7. Lead your team in a book study on *Leading Change* by John Kotter. Schedule regular meetings to discuss and apply the concepts in the book.

Reflect on Your Learning

- Where did you grow the most in this competency?
- What next step do you need to take to continue to grow in this competency?

About the Authors

MAC LAKE is a national consultant and training program expert whose passion is growing leaders for the local church. He was instrumental in building the church planter assessment and training process for the North American Mission Board. He has been featured in online training programs and speaks and leads seminars. Mac is the author of *The Multiplication Effect: Building a Leadership Pipeline That Solves Your Leadership Shortage*. A graduate of Moody Bible Institute and Dallas Theological Seminary, Mac and his wife, Cindy, live in Charleston, South Carolina. Mac blogs at maclakeonline.com and appears on YouTube at youtube.com/maclake. For more information on Mac's organization Multiply Group, visit multiplygroup.org.

RICK DUNCAN is the founding pastor of Cuyahoga Valley Church (CVC) just outside Cleveland, Ohio. Although he is still active in serving CVC, he led the church through a lead pastor succession plan in 2012. Since then, Rick has served with Mac Lake at the Send Network of the North American Mission Board as a member of the church planting training team and as the city missionary for Cleveland. Rick now coaches and consults church leaders in the areas of succession planning, transformational discipleship, and church multiplication. He has been married to Maryanne for forty-seven years, and they have three adult sons, Alan, Ryan, and Evan. You can reach Rick at rduncan@cvconline.org and follow him on Instagram @rickduncanlive.

CHECK OUT THE REST OF OUR DISCIPLING LEADERS SERIES

If you want more resources like *Leading an Organization* we have books for each level of leadership in your church or organization.

FIND MORE RESOURCES AT MULTIPLYGROUP.ORG

LET US HELP YOU TAKE YOUR NEXT STEP

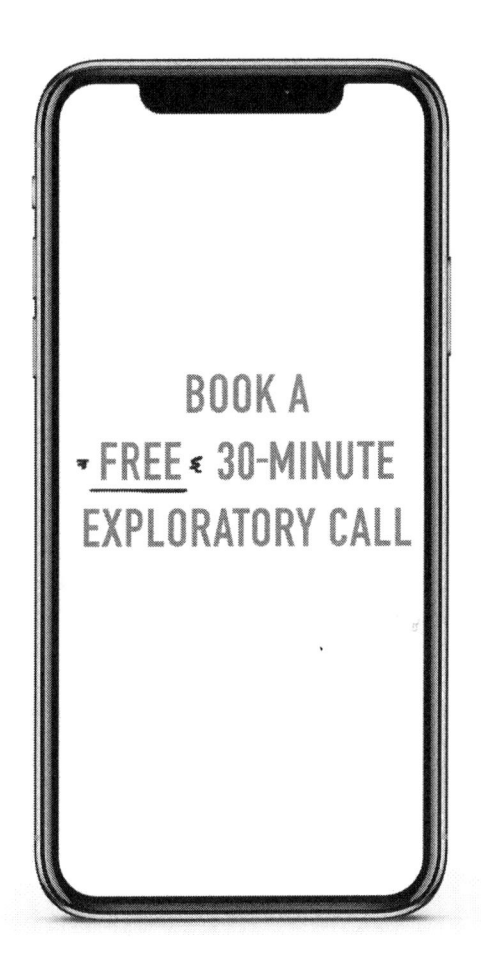

BOOK A FREE 30-MINUTE EXPLORATORY CALL

Would you like more information on how to develop leaders to take your ministry to the next level? We can help!

VISIT MULTIPLYGROUP.ORG/BOOK

DOWNLOAD OUR FREE GUIDE FOR PLANNING AND EXECUTING SUCCESSFUL INTERNSHIPS OR RESIDENCIES

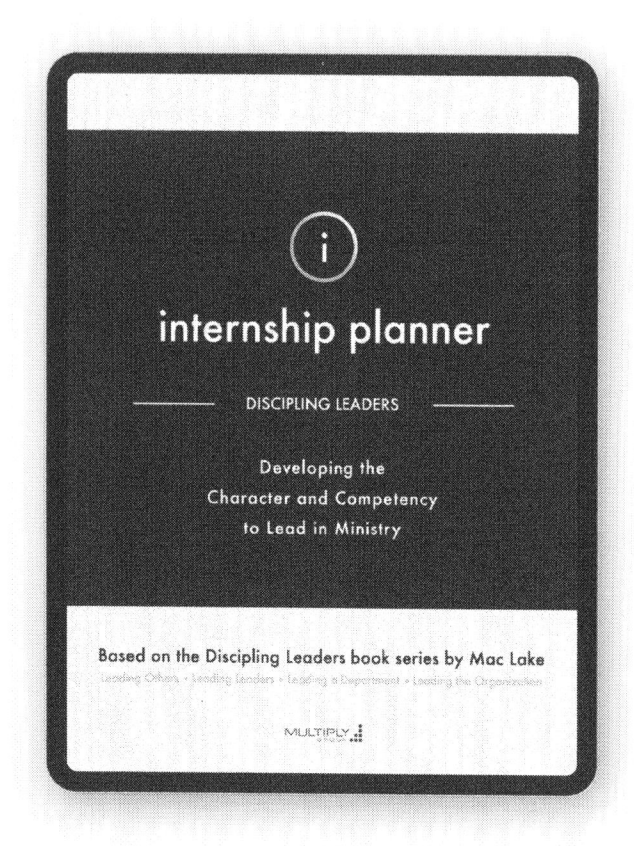

Get ministry interns up and running with the plug-and-play Internship Planner.

MULTIPLYGROUP.ORG/INTERNSHIP-PLANNER

DISCOVER HOW TO BUILD A STRATEGY TO SOLVE YOUR LEADERSHIP SHORTAGE

The Multiplication Effect reveals a practical, biblical, and proven strategy for addressing your leadership shortage and equipping future leaders to fulfill their kingdom mission.

This book will help you:
- Identify potential leaders using unique training modules
- Equip and disciple leaders at every level of their leadership journey
- Empower leaders to multiply themselves by developing other leaders

ORDER YOUR COPY TODAY AT MULTIPLYGROUP.ORG

Made in the USA
Columbia, SC
02 August 2024